Vignettes

AF816910

MAXFIELD PARRISH
THE ART PRINTS

Michael J. Goldberg

Collectors Press, Inc.
Portland, Oregon

Acknowledgements

Collection courtesy of Erwin Flacks, Fine Art Marketing Co., and the archives of Collectors Press, Inc.

Editor:
Michael J. Goldberg

Design:
Hoover H.Y. Li

Copyright © 1998 Collectors Press, Inc.

All rights reserved. No part of this book may be reproduced or transmitted in any form or by any means, electronic or mechanical, including photocopying, recording, or by any information storage and retrieval system, without written permission from Collectors Press, Inc.

Published by: Collectors Press, Inc.
P.O. Box 230986, Portland, OR 97281
1-800-423-1848

Printed in Singapore

First American Edition

10 9 8 7 6 5 4 3 2 1

ISBN: 1-888054-19-0

Maxfield Parrish

Utilizing their creative powers, many artists, writers, composers, et al., have bewitched us into distant times and lands – places found only in our deepest wishes and most wonderful dreams. As we close the door on the twentieth century we look back to see a man who opened the door at the beginning – who flooded our world with some of the most well-loved and nostalgic artwork in these last one hundred years.

Maxfield Parrish created his beautiful images of ethereal maidens and Mother Goose characters in a time when people were still capable of romanticizing the past in response to an ever encroaching

Land of Make-Believe
1912

twentieth century. Unlike Norman Rockwell, whose subjects were a product of the artist's nostalgia for a contemporary world as he wished it, Parrish evoked a nostalgia for a legendary world that was a mix of mythological, European, Oriental and Early American fantasies and subjects. In today's world, Maxfield Parrish's images are *still* as popular as when they were created. This cannot be said of many artists, even of fifty years vin-

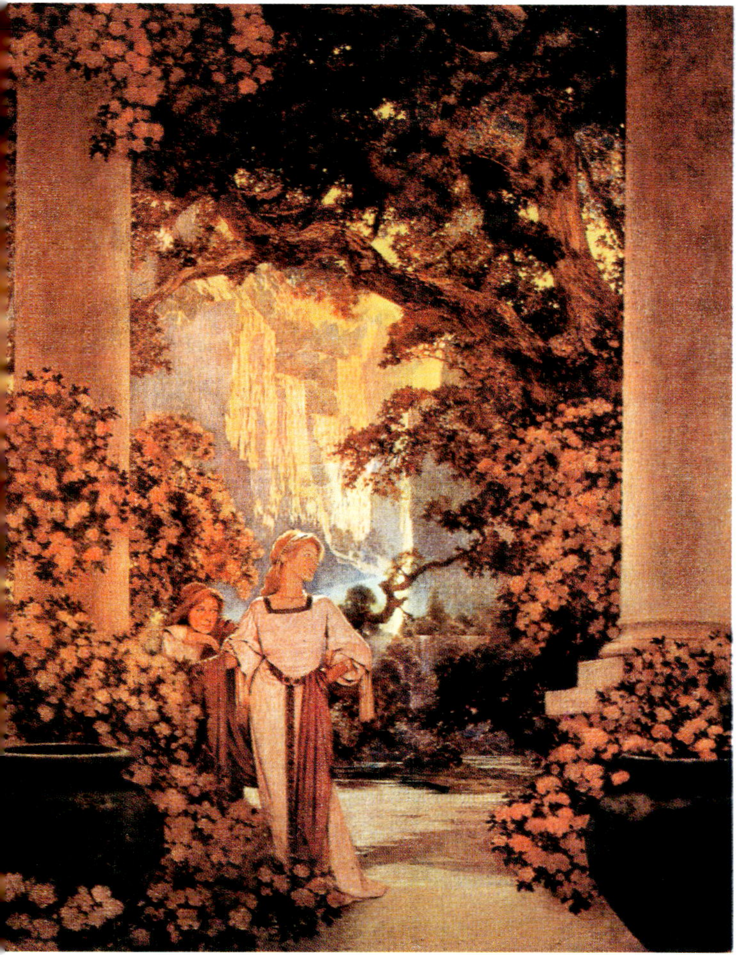

Cadmus Sowing the Dragon's Teeth
1909

tage. Not only is Parrish's work still prized, but many people, young and old, are actually familiar with different Parrish classics. His work has been raised to an almost iconographic level. As contemporary publishers reproduce Parrish images in the forms of books, calendars, trading cards, greeting cards, etc., they are eagerly bought by a public that seems to be insatiable for the Parrish persona. His name is more

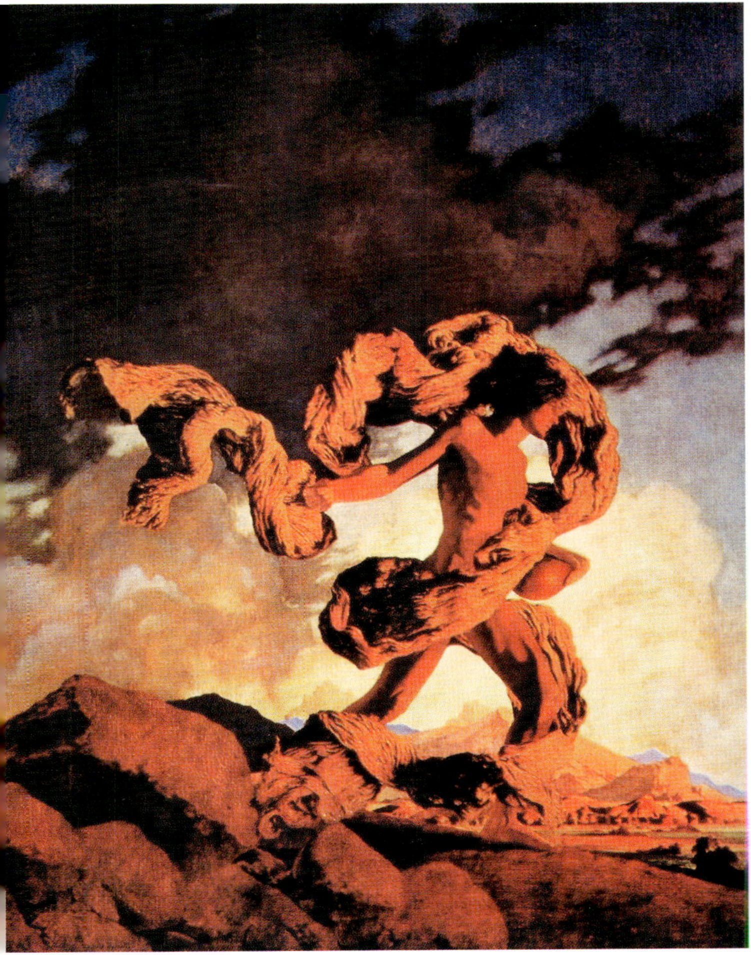

Wild Geese
1924

familiar to the public than most contemporary artists who struggle in a world where art is reduced to a commodity.

Parrish is more than profit though, he is also inspiration. In the late 1960s, young artists and designers felt that illustration (or any piece of fine art used in a commercial way) should still be considered art, a concept not particularly shared by the

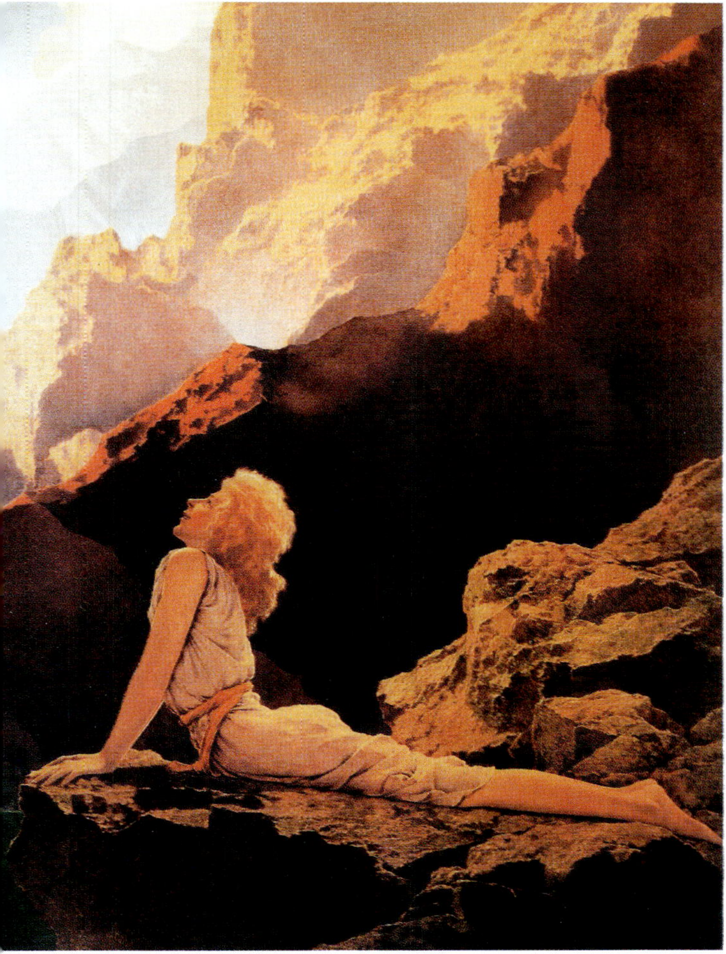

Queen Gulnare
1907

industry and quickly passed on to the eager public. In a counter-cultural move fueled by a new sense of nostalgia, these artists reached into the past to rediscover such artists as Parrish, as well as Aubrey Beardsley, Alphonse Mucha, M.C. Escher and others from the Art Nouveau Movement and the early twentieth century. These prototypal illustrators had attained a sort of "camp" romantic

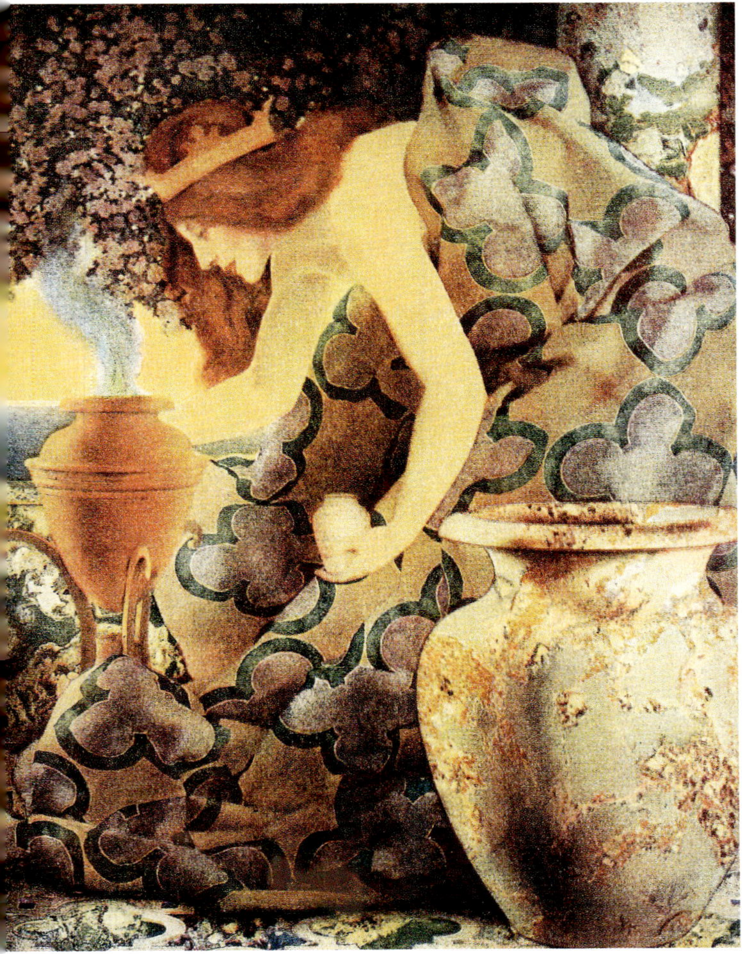

The Canyon
1924

status for these young artists and they were quickly inspired to borrow freely from the styles. Parrish offered them great composition, beautiful figures and, above all else, an exquisite color palette and color technique.

When Coy Ludwig's definitive 1973 book *Maxfield Parrish* was published, contemporary artists such as Palatino, Byrd, and David Goines were producing posters with decidedly

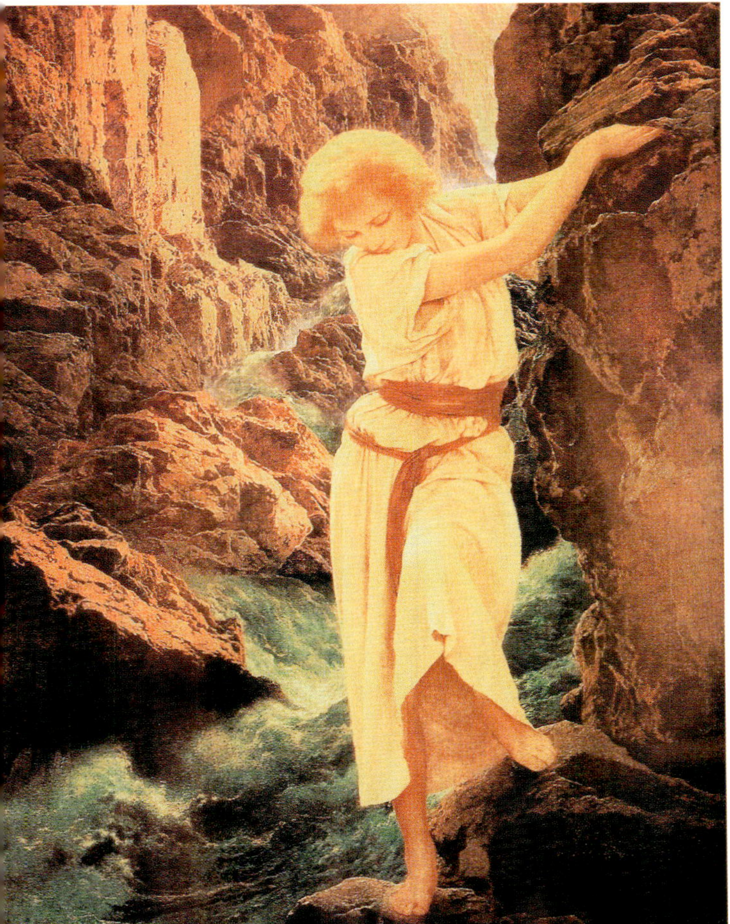

Evening
1922

Parrish influences that were being framed and hung as art. Posters had finally achieved the status of art and publishers were quick to see this fact. Reproductions of some of Parrish's well-known pieces appeared in print and poster forms and Ludwig's book had become the standard work on Parrish and has since enjoyed many reprintings.

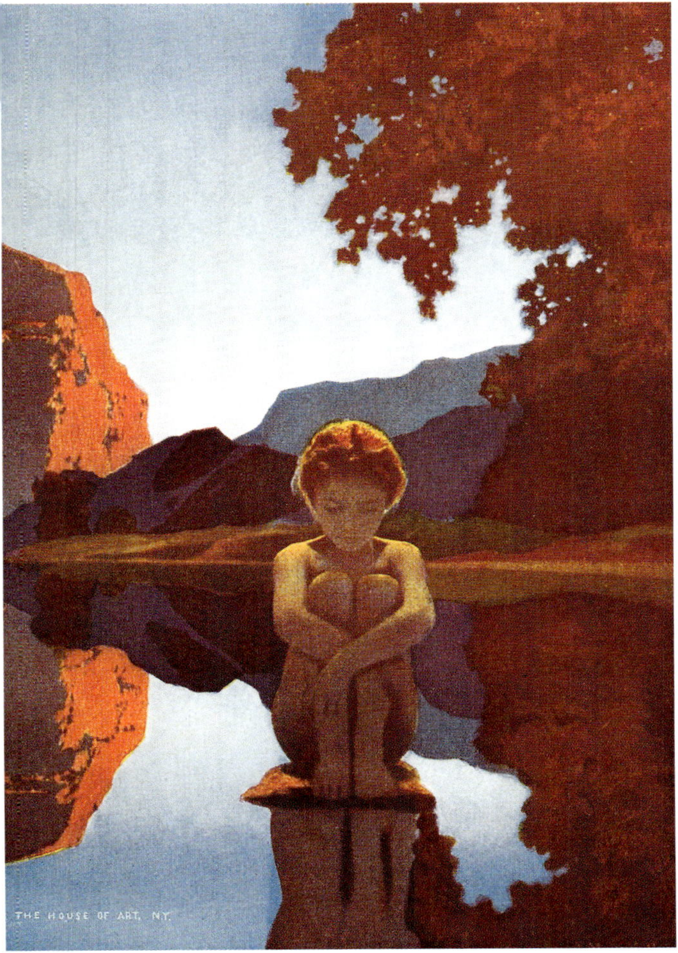
THE HOUSE OF ART, N.Y.

Morning
1922

The new interest in Parrish and his contemporaries also caught the interest of the painting and art print world. Young art and print collectors turned their attentions to the late nineteenth century and early twentieth century artists, where a vast field of incredible art lay waiting to be discovered. Parrish was a favorite, of course, as much of his work had survived and so much had been printed.

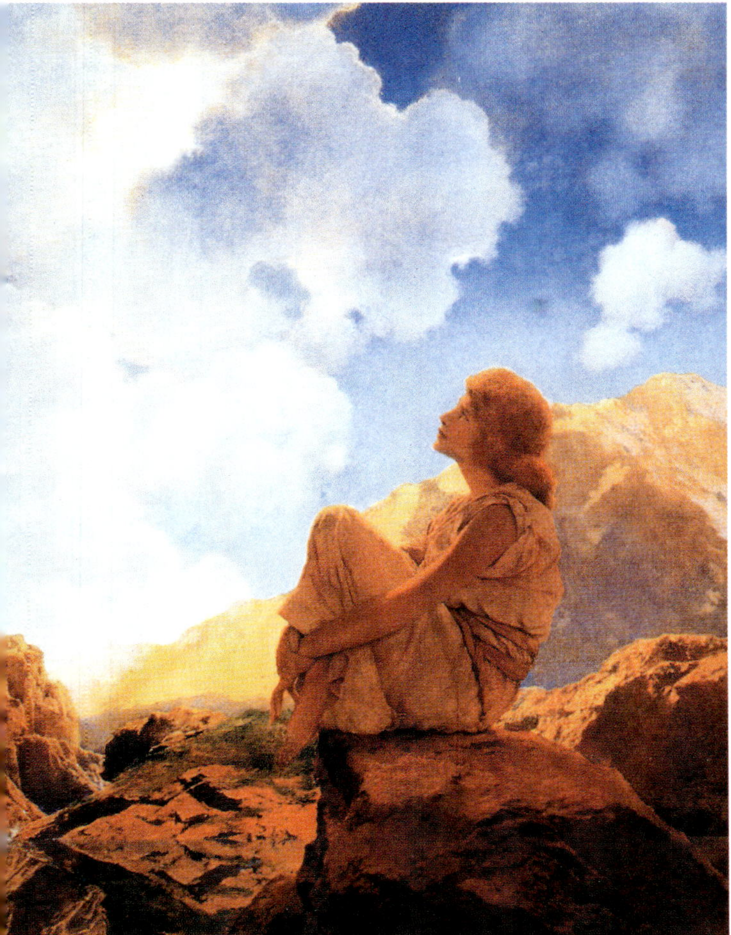

Dreaming
1928

In fact, young and eager collectors found that there was a love of Parrish's art that had never died. Even in the 1970s, many elderly people still had original framed prints of *Daybreak, Stars,* and *Garden of Allah* hanging in their homes.

As popular as he is today, Parrish was just as well loved in his own time and so was the art print in general. When Parrish was born in 1870, the

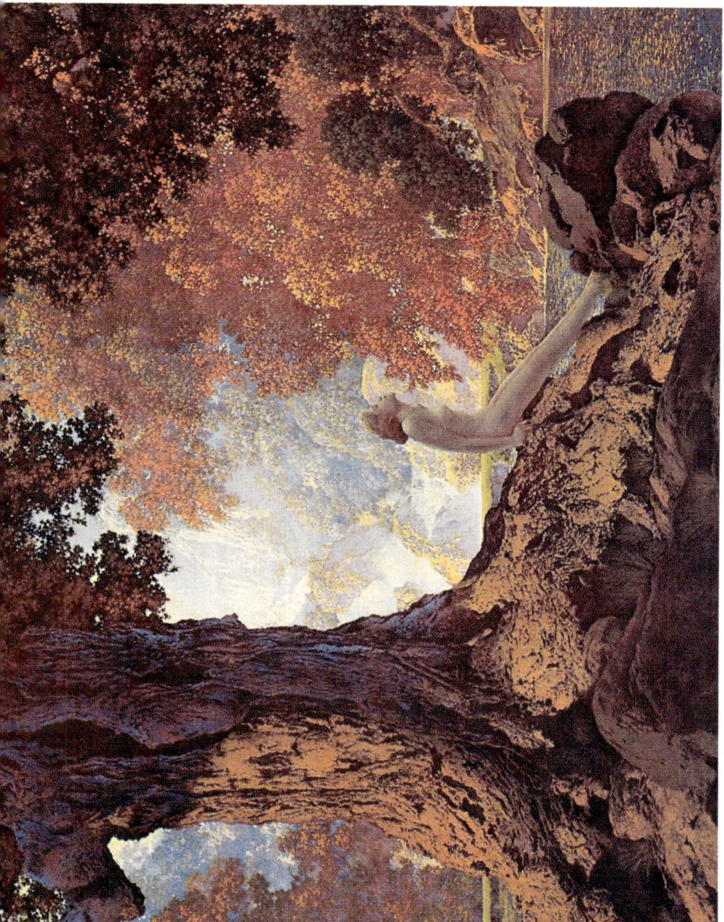

"art print" was also coming into existence. A by-product of the Industrial Revolution, the art print gave the average person a chance of owning good quality versions of famous paintings – art having been originally only the province of the rich. Advanced technology in the printing fields over the next fifty years had brought lithographic, photographic, and color standards up to new levels of quality. The

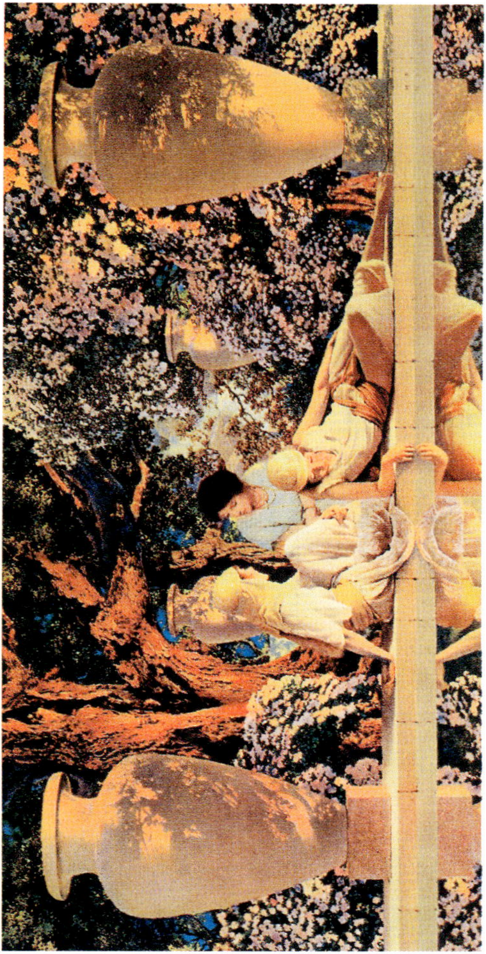

Pierrot's Serenade
1908

public's demand for more art created an art print market which drew many romantic souls to its ranks. A new art venue was born whereby an artist's work could be viewed by vast numbers of people. Out of the hundreds of artists who contributed to the art print market, only a handful achieved celebrity status or acquired considerable wealth. This required, among other things, for an artist to have a

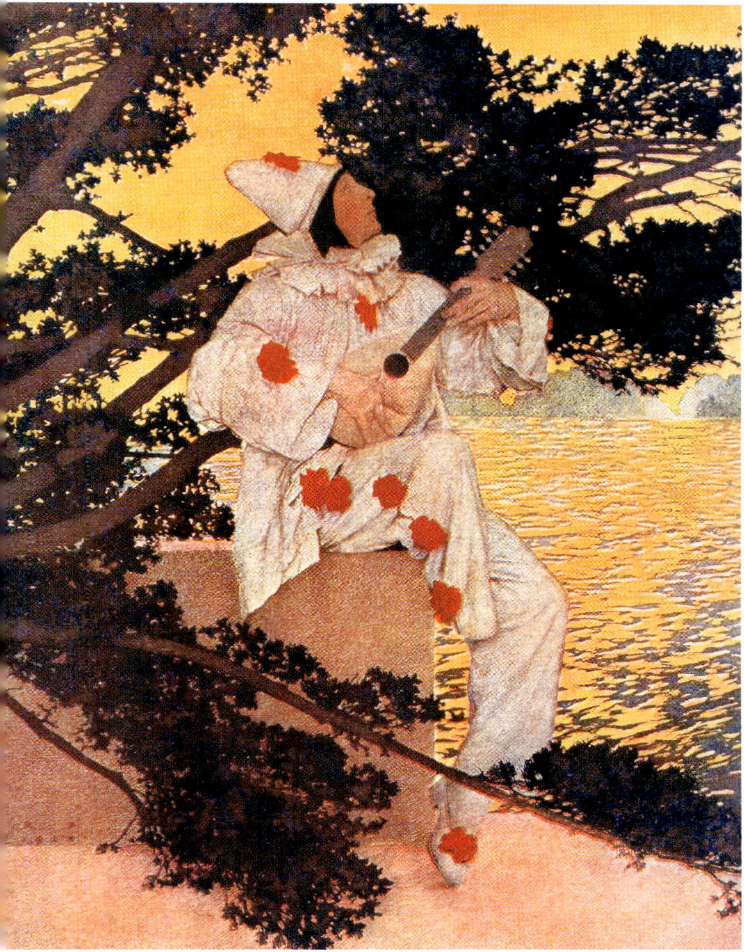

very good sense of what the public demanded and a highly attractive, noticeable style. Fortunately for Parrish, he had both.

Parrish's first art prints appeared in 1904. They were reproductions of covers he had done for the *Ladies' Home Journal* and were sold through the magazine by mail order. These sold well enough that Charles Scribner's Sons, the publisher for

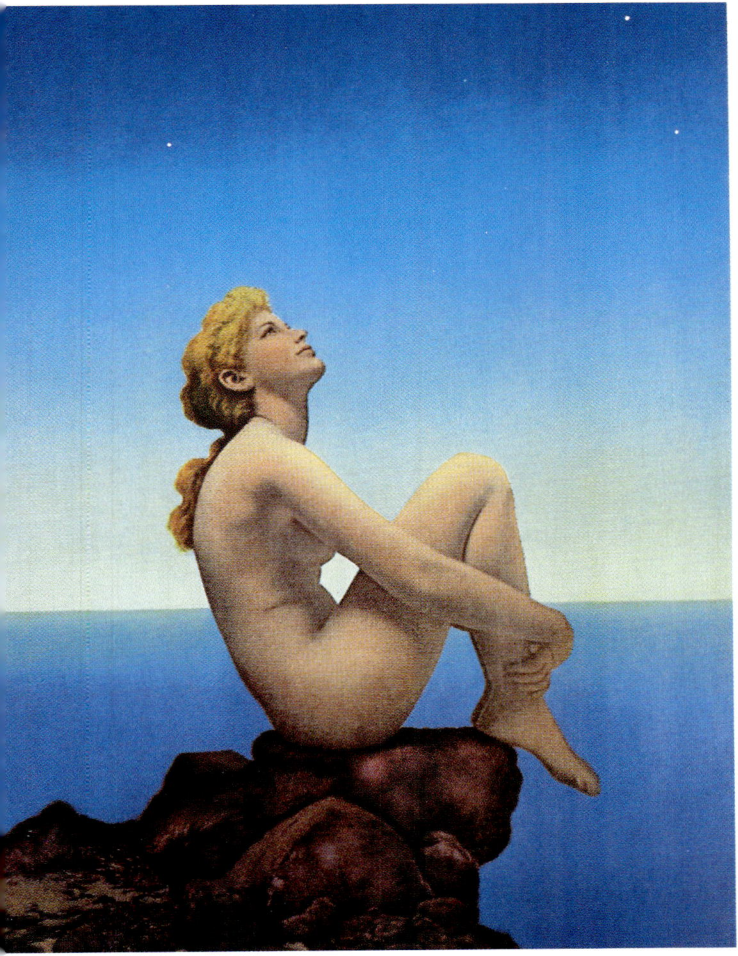

whom Parrish did book illustrations, offered art prints of four illustrations the artist did for Eugene Field's *Poems of Childhood*. The enthusiastic reception for these prints led Scribner's to reproduce more illustrations from that book.

Curiously, very few Parrish "prints" would appear until 1916. It was in that year that Parrish completed a commission that would eventually

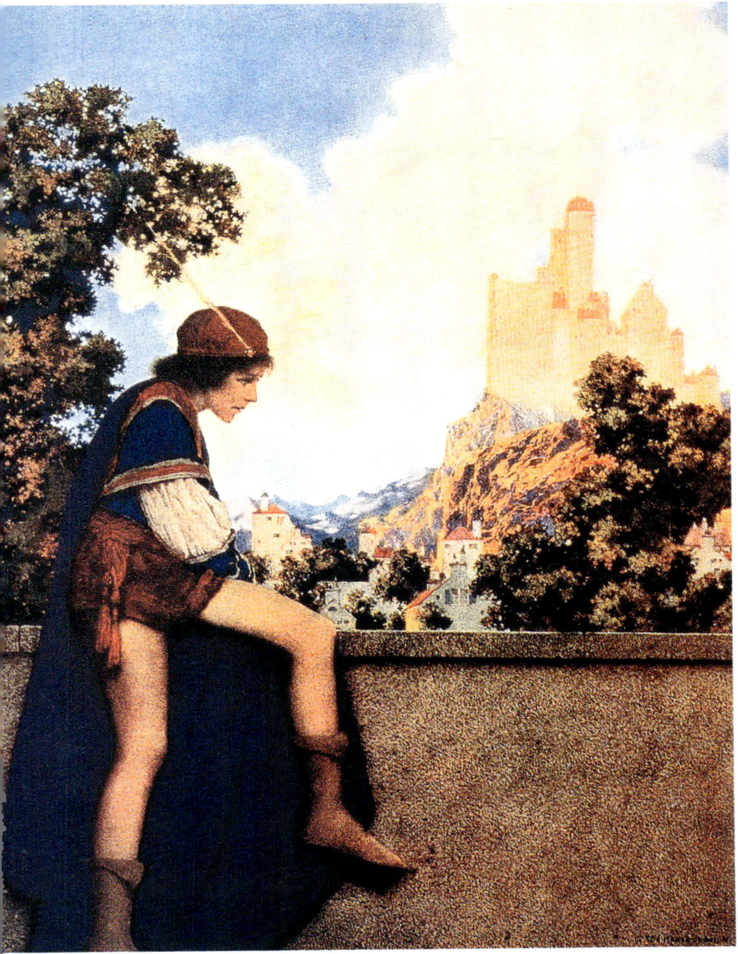

lead him to create his most famous print works. A gentleman named Clarence Crane, who owned Crane's Chocolates, approached Parrish to design a logo for the gift boxes that held his candy. Parrish's small decoration showing a crane (the bird) pleased Crane immensely and he commissioned Parrish to create a painting for the decoration of the 1916 Christmas gift box. Crane

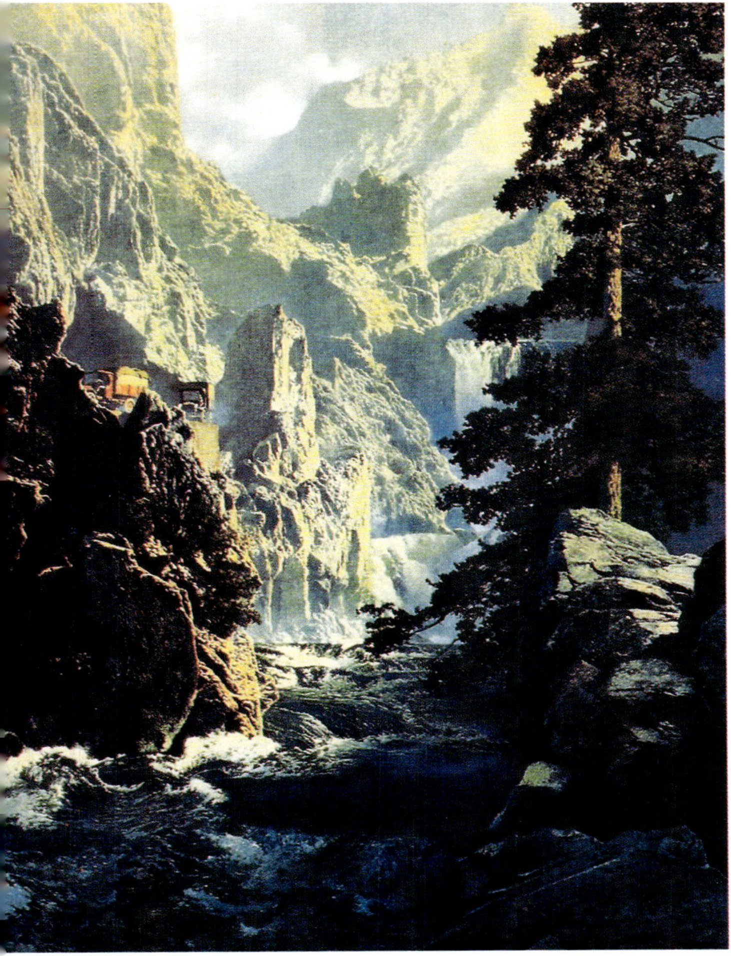

Daybreak
1923

requested the subject to be the Rubaiyat of Omar Khayyam. Parrish created the beautiful and well-known *Rubaiyat,* redolent in visual splendor and Parrish's trademarks: the reposed maiden, shadowing trees, and panoramic, color drenched scenery. (Both the artist and client considered the idea of placing a box of Crane's chocolates in the scene – fortunately it was dropped.)

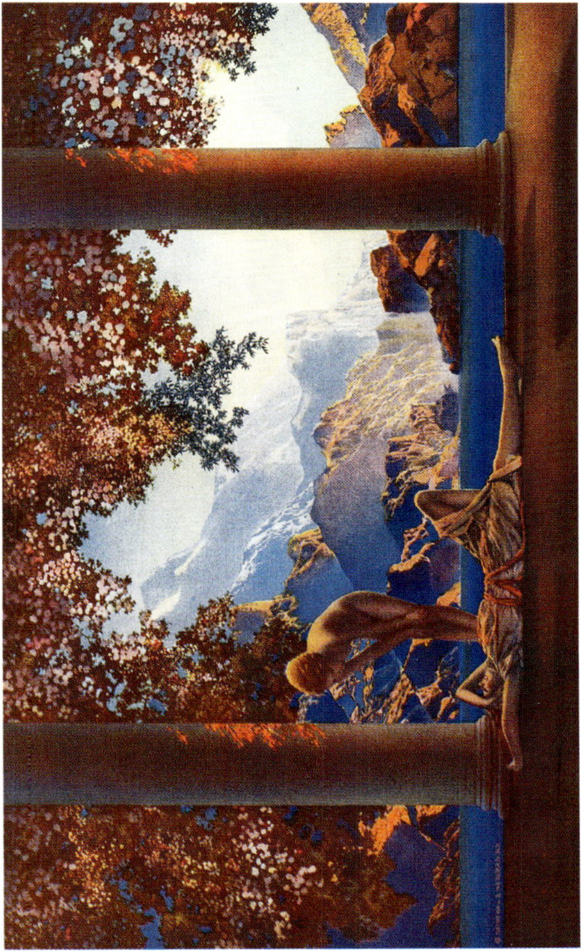

The Prince
1925

When Crane received the original painting in mid-1916, he was so inspired he decided to have prints made not only for the box, but to also have full-sized prints of *Rubaiyat* made and available through a mail order coupon in each box of chocolates. This early example of marketing wizardry produced an instant burst of public enthusiasm. With this success, Crane requested a box for 1917. Parrish delivered another piece

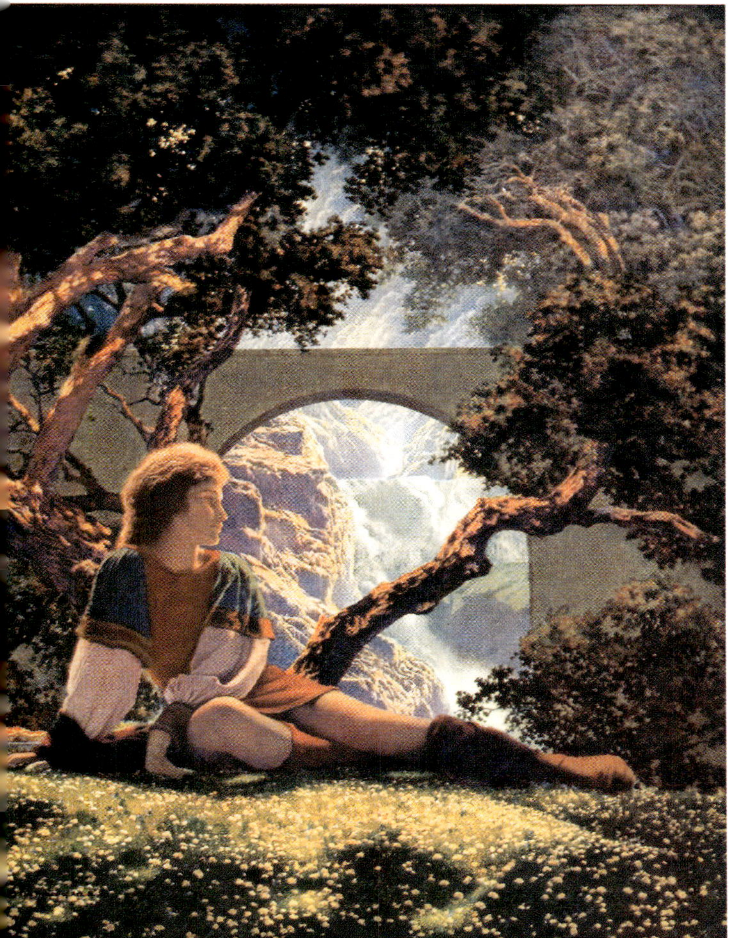

Air Castles
1904

of his brand of exotica with the painting *Cleopatra*, featuring an flapperish-looking Cleo on her barge with servants in attendance. This also met with much popularity, but Parrish was tired of doing advertising. Having to paint what other people dictated was not how he envisioned his art career. This highly particular artist found a chance to achieve his goal when the fine art publishing firm, the House of Art (who was at

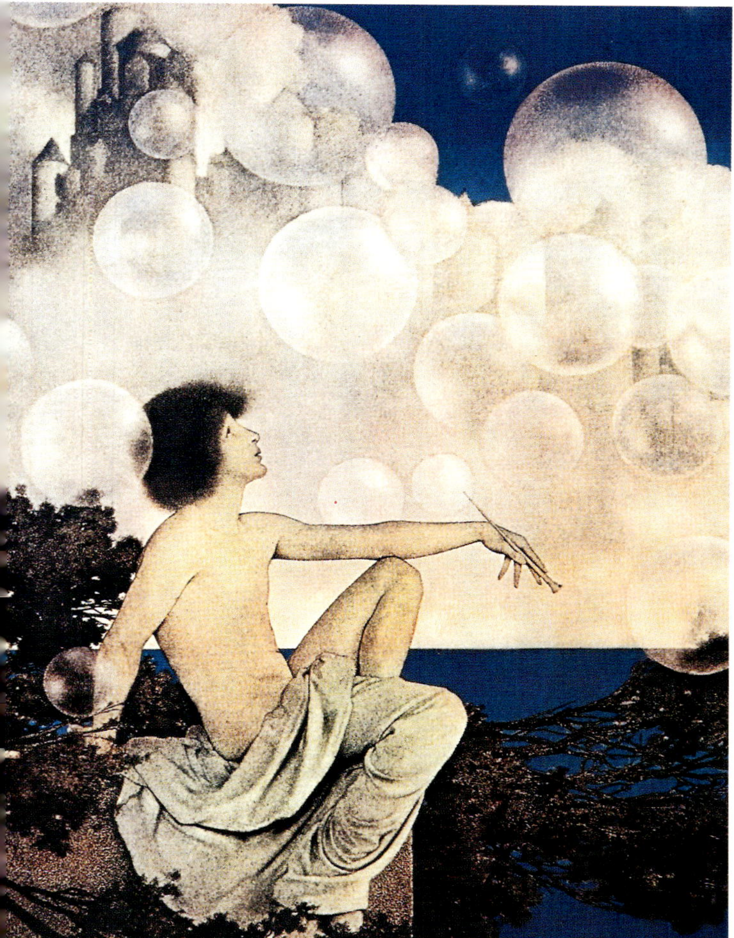

The Dinkey-Bird
1905

the time marketing Parrish's art prints for Crane) asked him to create images specifically for them to reproduce and market. Better yet, the picture subject could be the artist's choice. Though Crane made a huge offer for the next gift box design, *Garden of Allah* would be the last piece Parrish would produce for Crane's Chocolates. Sales of the reproductions of the art prints skyrocketed and Parrish moved on with confidence.

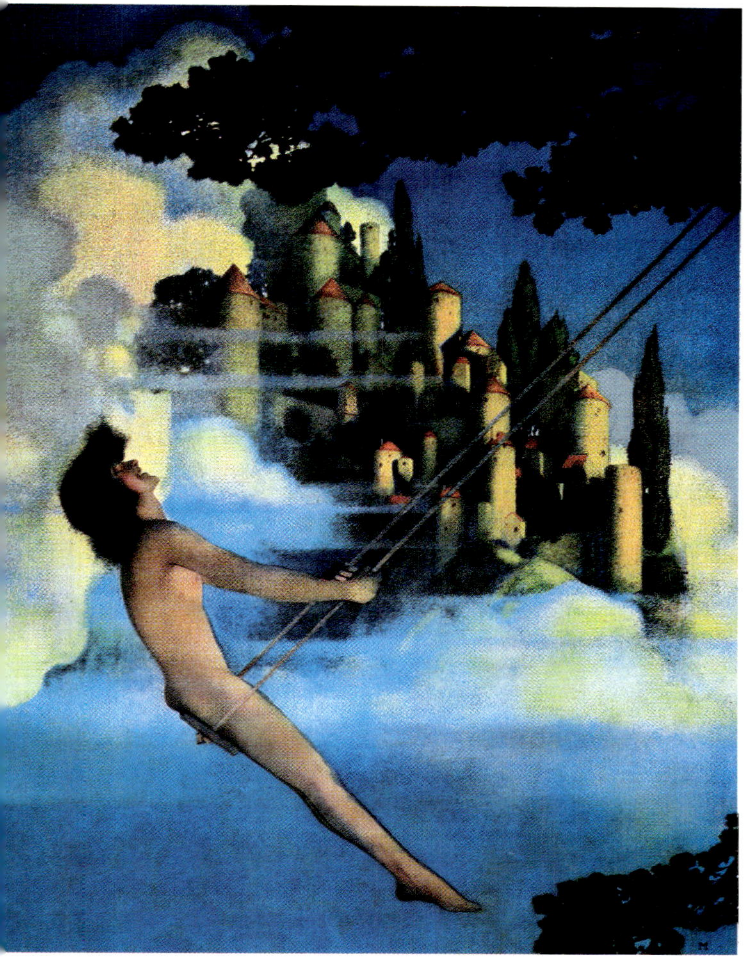

Wynken, Blynken and Nod
1905

The House of Art immediately began turning some of Parrish's magazine covers and other works into saleable art prints. It was not until 1923 that Parrish created the first piece specifically for the House of Art. Inspired by the success of *Garden of Allah,* Parrish strove to recreate a similar but unique vision. For this Parrish would sweep together all the images to create this landmark piece: majestic, piercing mountains, dramatic

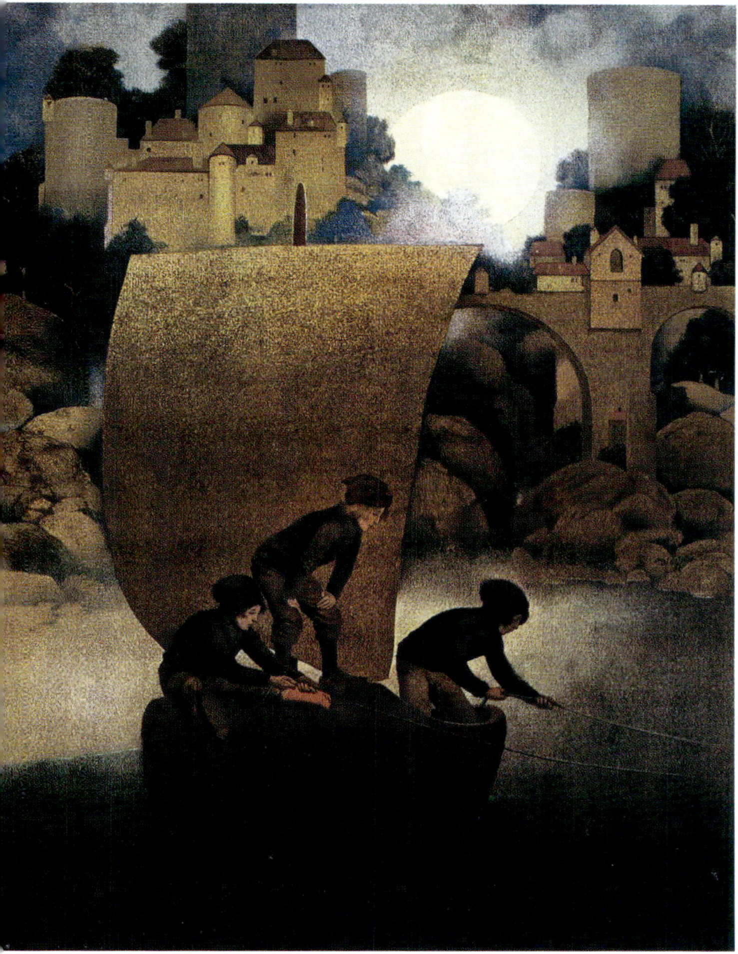

sweeping clouds, twilight blue skies, and Neo-Romantic young women in diaphanous gowns (or sometimes unclothed, like in the print *Stars*), lazily languishing amid Greco-Romanesque or Far Eastern architecture. The print, titled *Daybreak,* was finally offered in the fall of 1923. Neither the artist nor the publisher was ready for the incredible popularity of the piece. You might even say there was a "craze" for *Daybreak* at

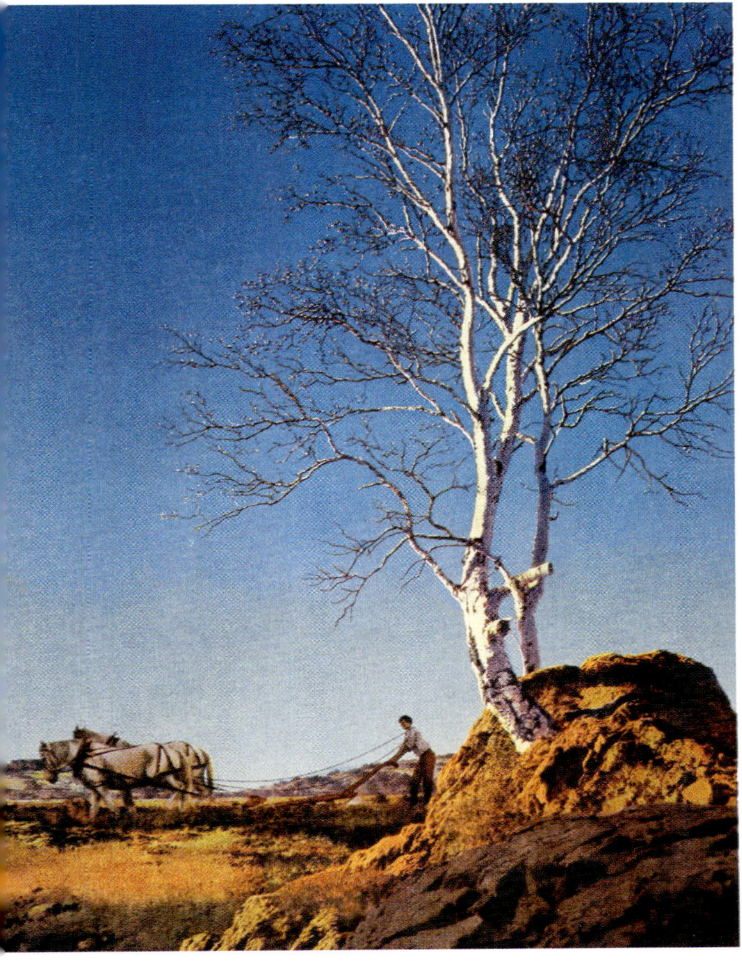

one point. It became *the* giftware item of the day and everyone from grad students to grannies bought one. The popularity of *Daybreak* was so far reaching that it stretched from the consumer into the art field. Throngs of young illustrators and artists offered their variation on *Daybreak's* theme, along with a multitude of exotic gardens, enchanted isles and classical settings. Many were, at best, mediocre attempts.

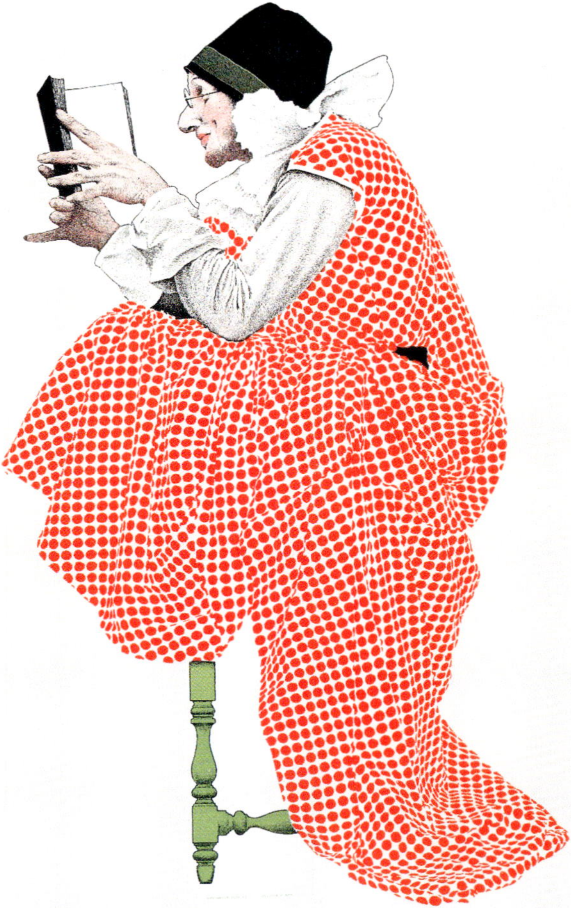

Prince Codadad
1906

Over the next year or so, the House of Art continued to reproduce older Parrish works which had not been seen before on such mass scales. The phenomenal success of *Daybreak* encouraged the House of Art to press Parrish into creating another *Daybreak*-like blockbuster. Parrish submitted two new paintings for reproduction: *Stars* and *Hilltop*. *Stars* featured a nude female figure sitting

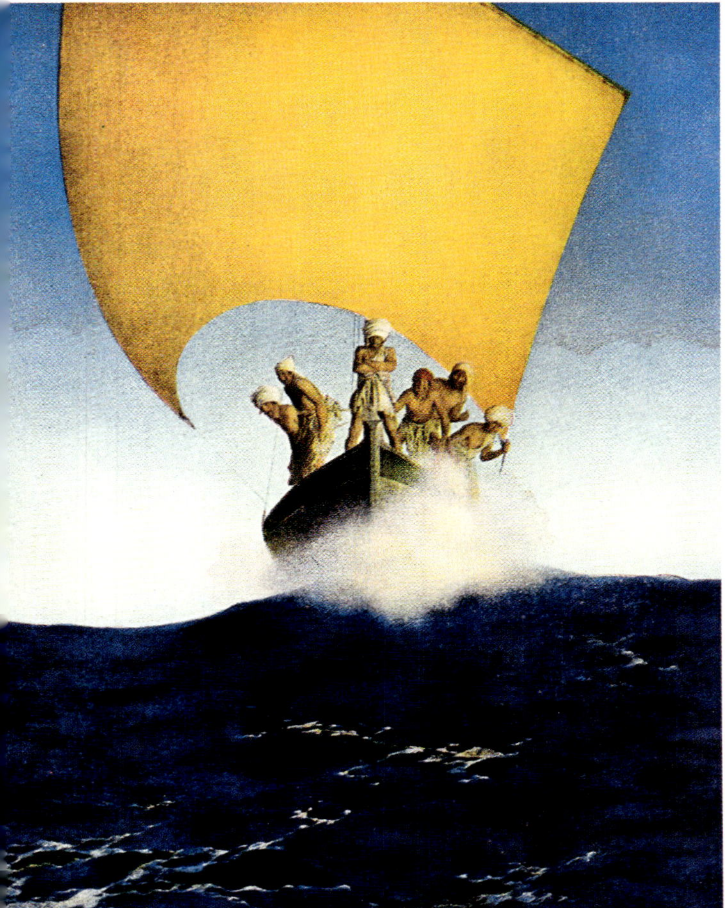

Jason and His Teacher
1910

perched on a high crag with just sea and sky in the background, and *Hilltop* shows two maidens sprawled under a shadowing tree atop a hill. These two pieces of work became available to the public in 1926. Their sales were not as spectacular as *Daybreak,* though they still made a substantial profit for both artist and publisher. The last collaboration between Parrish and the House of

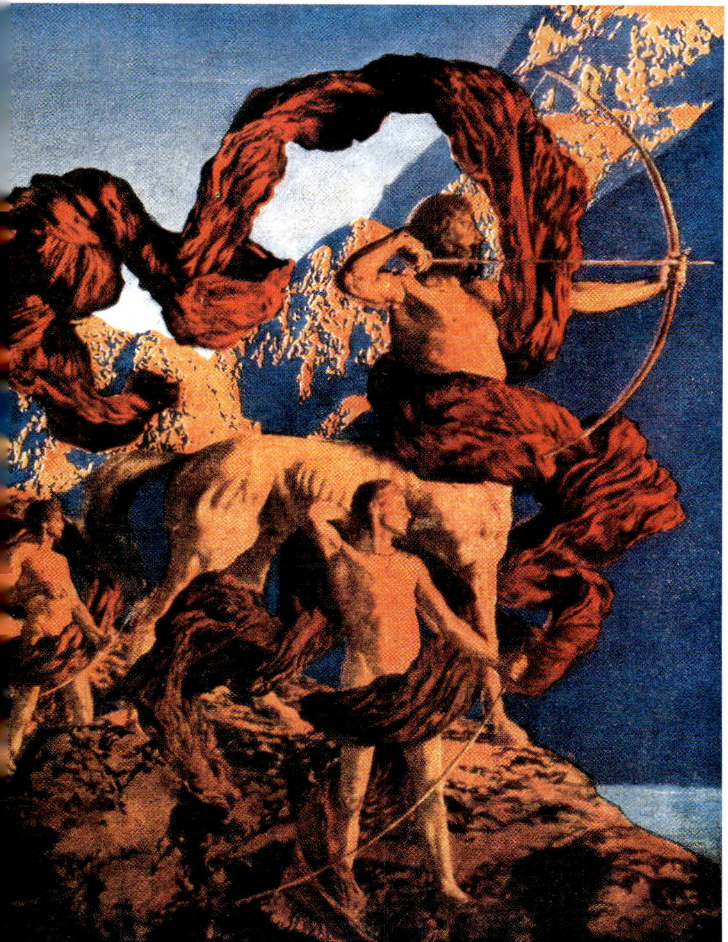

Hilltop
1921

Art came with the release of *Dreaming* (also called *October*) in 1928. *Dreaming* was, in fact, basically a landscape painting (which was the artist's aspiring field) showing a Parrishesque wooded river setting featuring a large, ancient tree in the foreground and a nude figure seated on one of its gnarled roots. The figure was added only at the request of the publishers, who felt that it was needed for "sales" purposes.

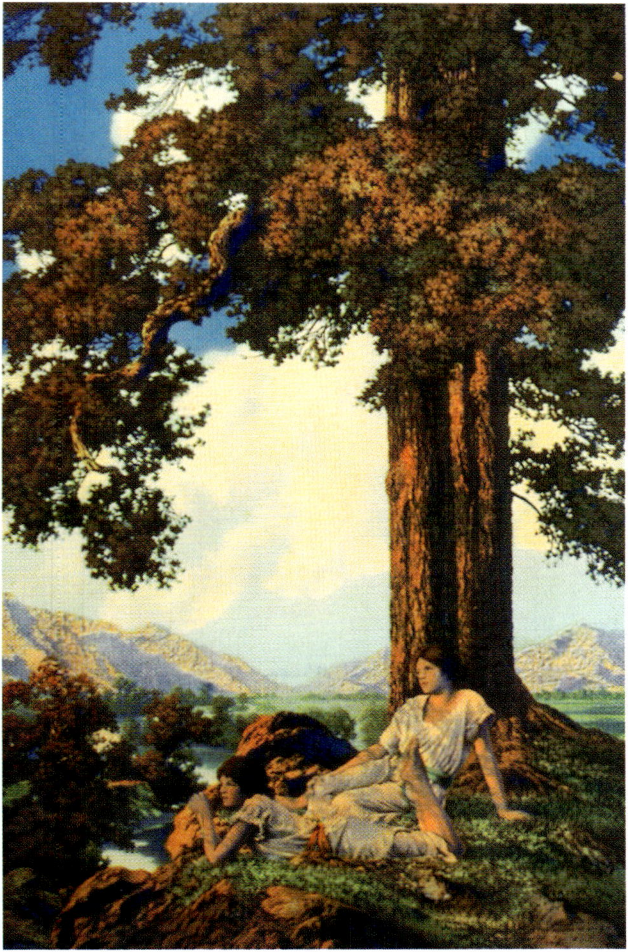

Interlude
1924

By 1930, Parrish had become disgusted by the demands of the art print field to dictate the images which he wanted to paint – not an unusual feeling for many artists. With sales of *Dreaming* dropping off, it became clear for the artist to make another move. The *Daybreak* craze was mostly over – the images of languid, innocent feminine beauty in bucolic landscapes so dear ten years ago were giving way to platinum blonde pin-

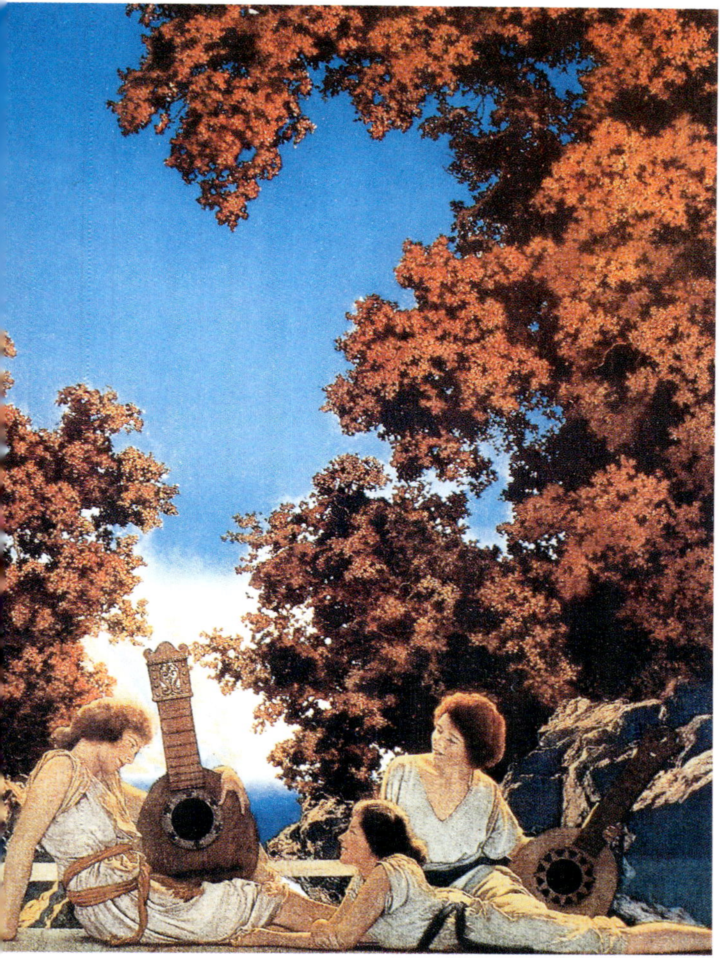

Sinbad Plots Against the Giant
1907

ups, Hollywood starlets, and cultured gardens. The pressure to create another *Daybreak* seemed ludicrous. Though all dealings between Parrish and the House of Art were over, the publishing firm continued to sell art prints of many of Parrish's most appealing works for years to come.

Parrish was able to turn his back on the genre-infested world of art prints when the calendar company

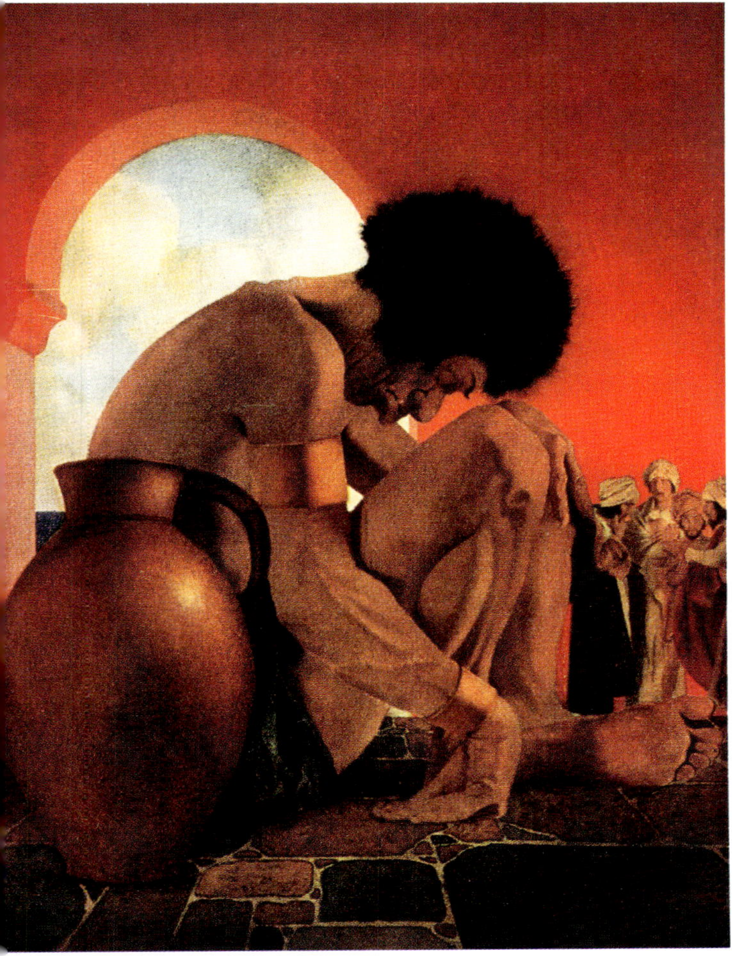

King of the Black Isles
1907

Brown & Bigelow offered to let Parrish paint landscapes for their calendars. Parrish was at first reluctant, already contributing art for General Electric's Edison Mazda line. But the idea of landscape painting with relative freedom of subject was too enticing. After his last calendar for General Electric in 1934, Parrish accepted the offer from Brown & Bigelow to provide one landscape a

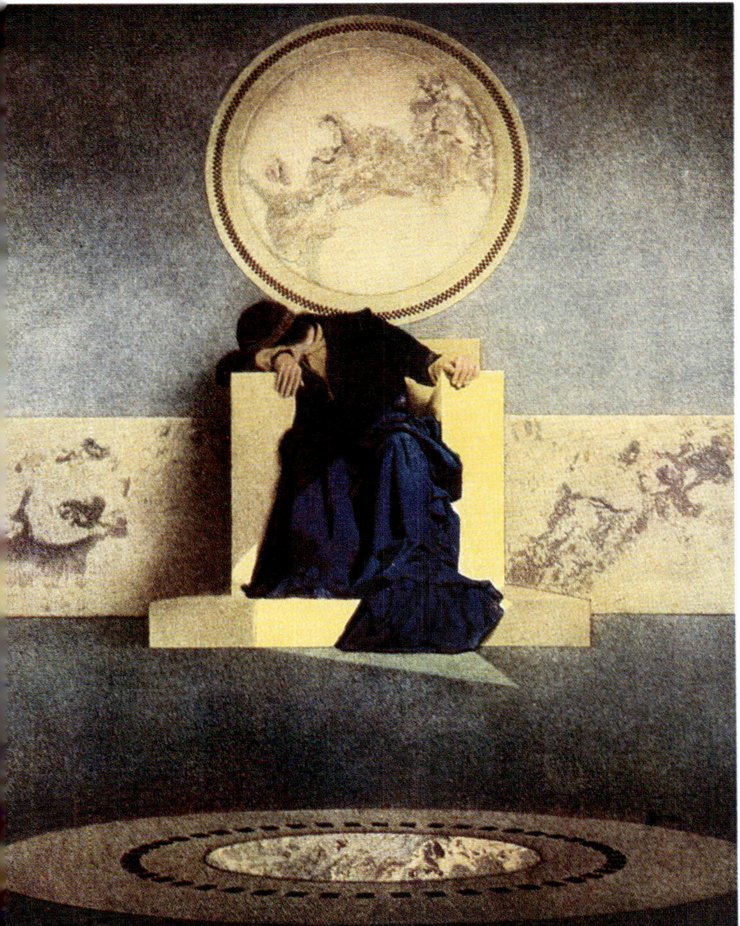

Pandora
1909

year for use on calendars. This series ran from 1936 to 1963 and included winter landscapes for greeting cards and small calendars. The evocative landscapes, with titles such as *Twilight, The Old Mill Pond,* and *Tranquility,* would employ all of Parrish's painting and color techniques on more realistic and serene images than his fantasy work of the past. He would never return to commercial art as a

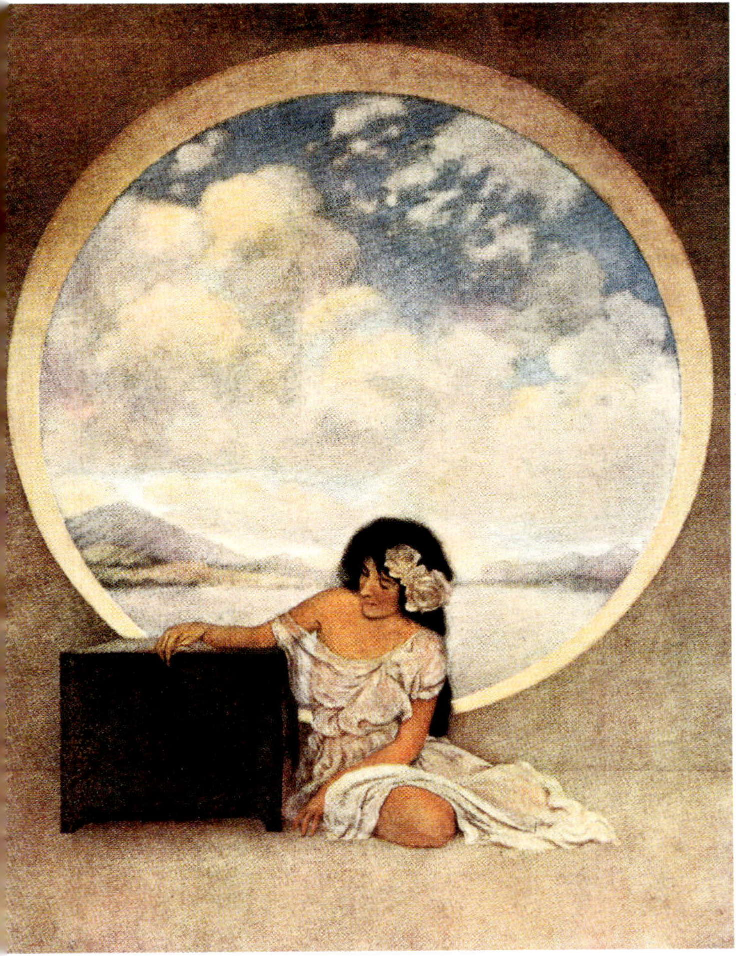

Harvest
1905

steady diet. Parrish stopped painting in 1962 at the age of 91. He died three years later at his home in Cornish, New Hampshire, where he had lived most of his adult life.

Today the name of Maxfield Parrish has become so entrenched in the American psyche that the phrases "a Parrish sunset" and "a Parrish maiden" conjure up specific images in

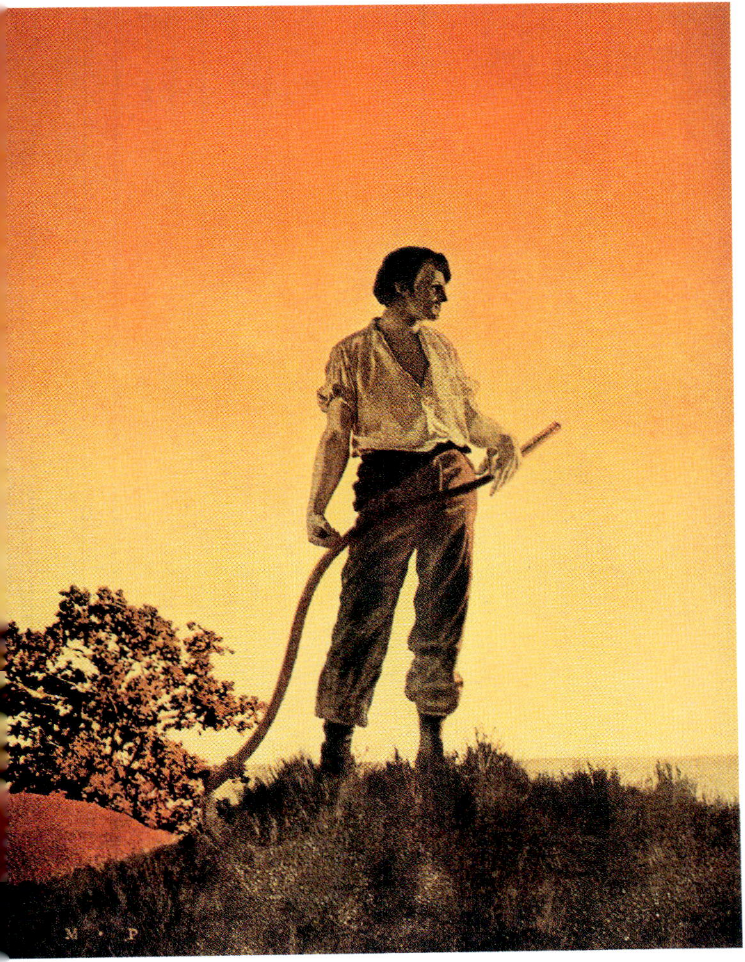
M · P

The Lantern Bearers
1910

everyone's mind of the work and style of this country's most beloved illustrator. His use of color was so unique that the beautiful blue he created for his skies has come to be referred to as "Parrish Blue."

Maxfield Parrish's star is not likely to dim in the near future. Reprints of his incredible art can be found in books, posters, postcards, and even trading cards. Interest in

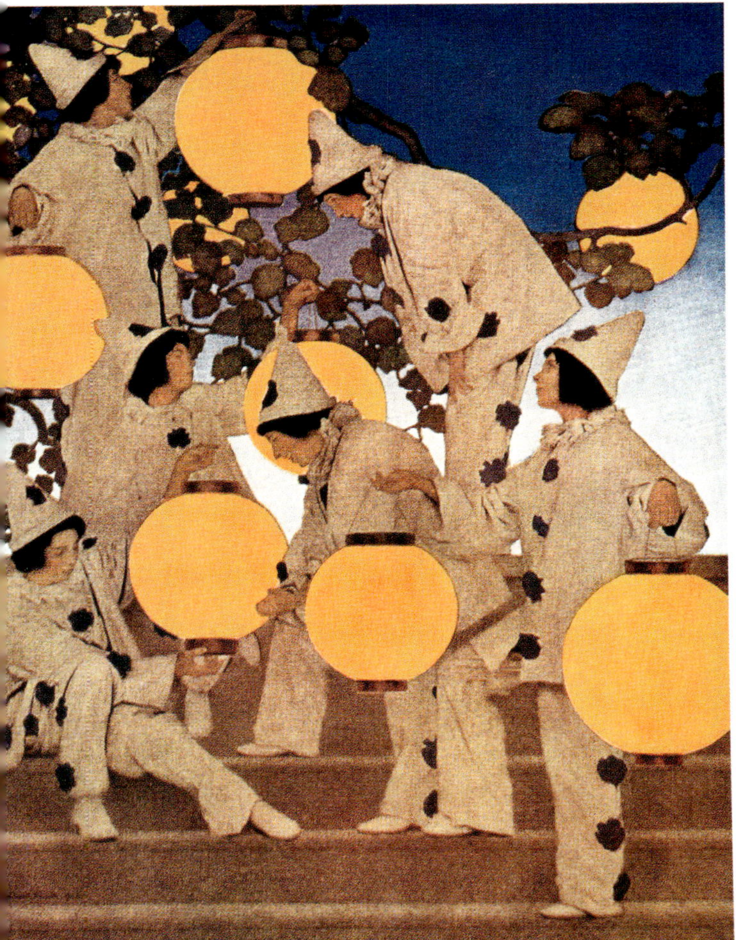

Sugar-Plum Tree
1905

the artist's original prints and calendars has grown into a legitimate field of collecting. New collectors stand in awe as they discover why many before them keep returning to Parrish – because his work is stunningly beautiful and can truly be called the pinnacle of the art print in the earlier twentieth century.

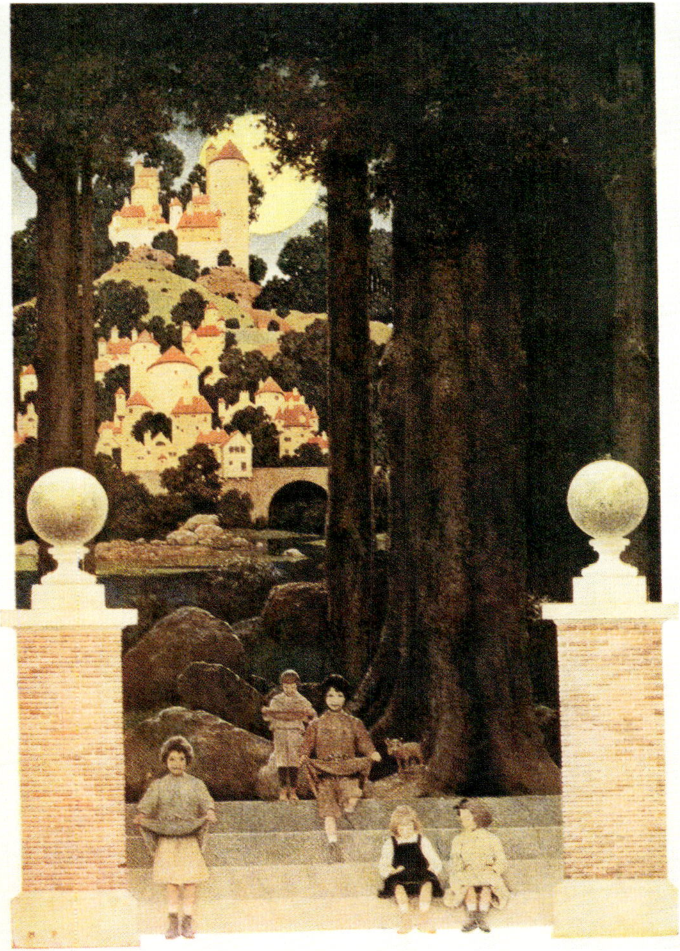

Vignettes

Vignettes

Vignettes Vignettes

Vignettes

Vignettes Vignettes

Vignettes

Vignettes Vignettes

Vignettes

Vignettes Vignettes

Vignettes

Vignettes Vignettes

Vignettes

Vignettes

MAXFIELD PARRISH

THE ADVERTISEMENTS

Michael J. Goldberg

Collectors Press, Inc.
Portland, Oregon

Acknowledgements

Collection courtesy of Erwin Flacks, Fine Art Marketing Co., and the archives of Collectors Press, Inc.

Editor:
Michael J. Goldberg

Design:
Hoover H.Y. Li

Copyright © 1998 Collectors Press, Inc.

All rights reserved. No part of this book may be reproduced or transmitted in any form or by any means, electronic or mechanical, including photocopying, recording, or by any information storage and retrieval system, without written permission from Collectors Press, Inc.

Published by: Collectors Press, Inc.
P.O. Box 230986, Portland, OR 97281
1-800-423-1848

Printed in Singapore

First American Edition

10 9 8 7 6 5 4 3 2 1

ISBN: 1-888054-20-4

Maxfield Parrish

The field of commercial art has long taken a back seat in the greater scope of artistic endeavors. In the Golden Age of Illustration (roughly the early twentieth century), all forms of commercial art – from greeting cards and package design to advertising and magazine illustrations – were highly embellished by today's standards and considered "pretty," a convenient way to enliven up a product or sell a magazine.

A few exceptional pieces managed to escape categorization and become "art" prints, among them Maxfield Parrish's works. Many artists who contributed visually to our work-a-day world over the

Dawn
1918

years, however, simply produced and were gone. Their legacies can be found on calendars, soap boxes, playing cards, posters, orange-crate labels, jigsaw puzzles, movie posters, and between the covers of countless magazines and books.

The *art* of commercial art did not become seriously appreciated until the 1960s. During this time of social

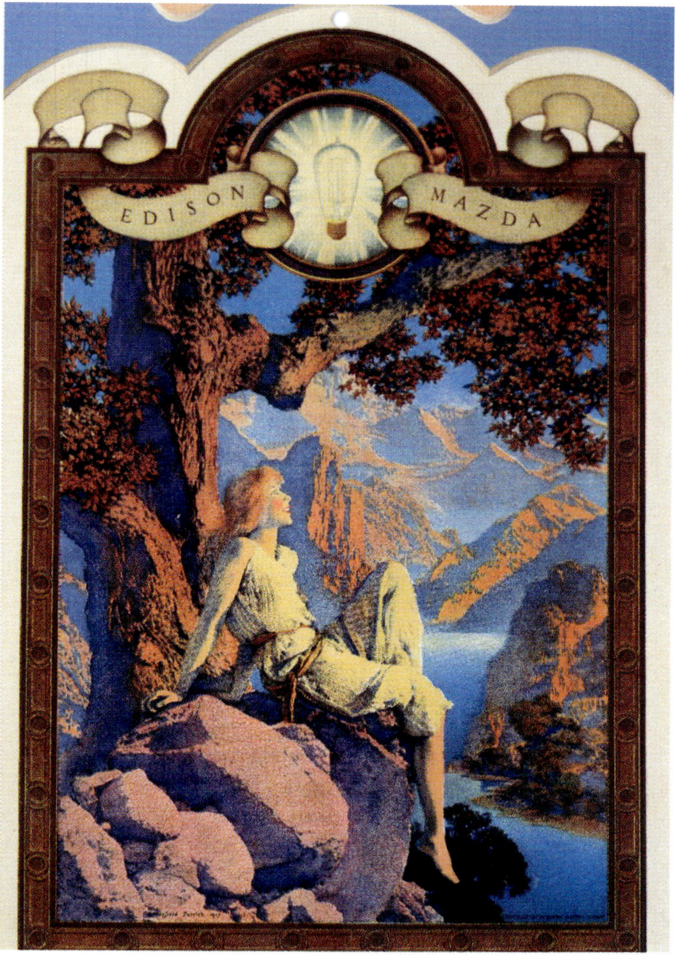
EDISON
MAZDA

upheaval, the Pop Artists appeared. Prompted by their personal visions and protests that fine art had become effete and beyond the average viewer's range, Pop Artists forced us to see everyday items as art. Both camp and serious, Pop Art led the way for many commercial art forms – posters, advertisements, book illustrations, comic books – to enjoy a new scrutiny and a stamp of artistic approval.

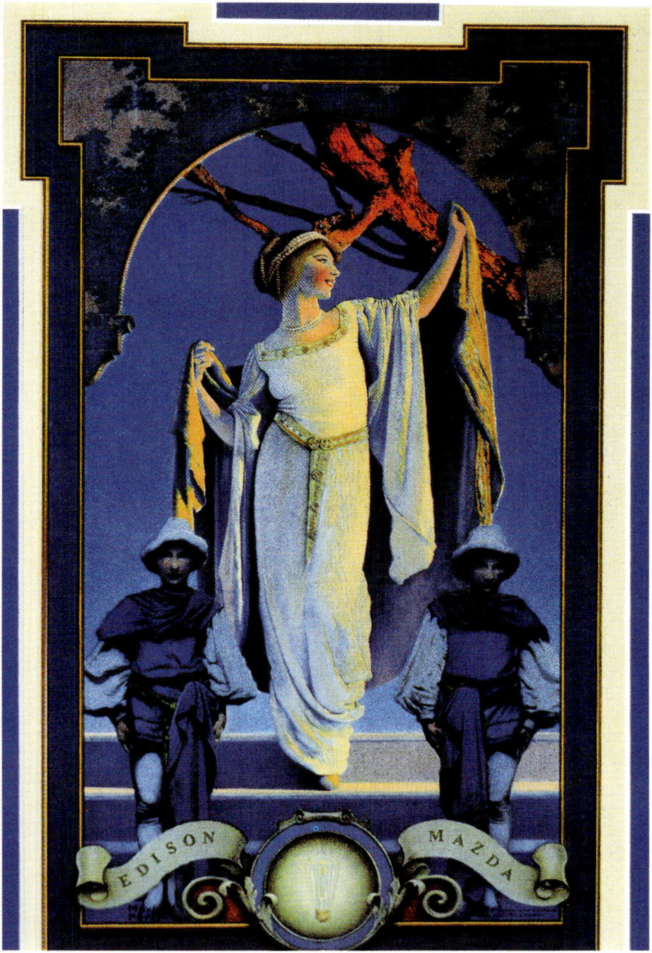
EDISON
MAZDA

A good example is comic art. Pop Artists like Roy Lichtenstein took single panels out of old comic strips, blew them up and hung them on walls. A panel from a comic strip or a soup can from the grocery shelf, taken out of context, develops a life of its own. Once a utilitarian form of entertainment, comic books and comic strips are collected today not only for the

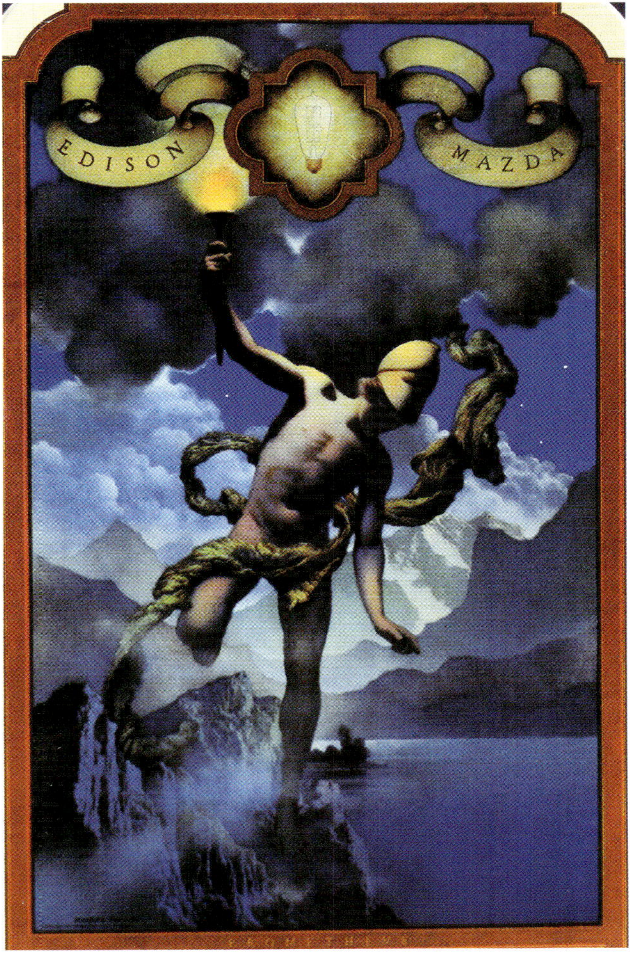
EDISON
MAZDA

stories but the artwork, as well. Prominent comic illustrators are celebrities in their field and are considered artists with a capital "A." Today we almost take the comic art form for granted, smug in our approval of its artistic merits.

Even more popular than comic art are many of the better examples of printed design and illustration, which

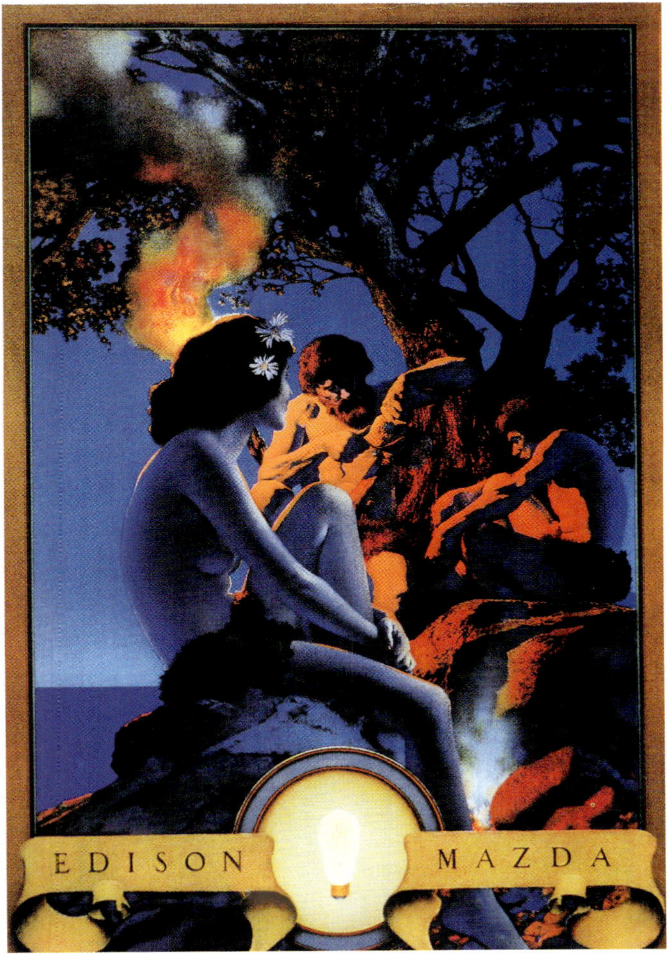
EDISON
MAZDA

Egypt
1922

are now appreciated as a familiar art form. None has been more universally embraced than work from the Golden Age of Illustration.

From the late 1800s to the early 1900s, technology improved greatly. Advances such as high-quality color reproduction and faster printing presses meant more and better books for a wider and increasingly discern-

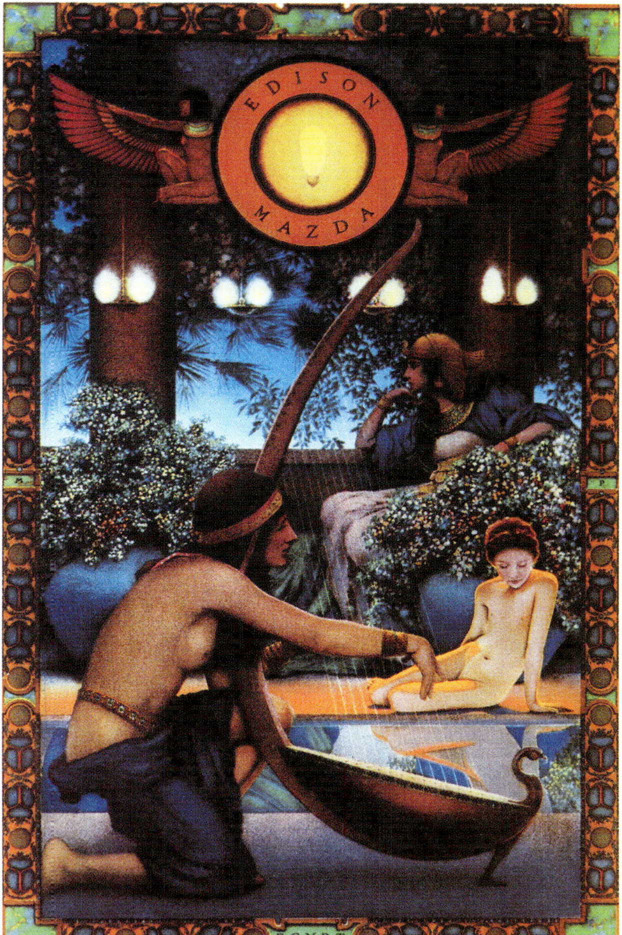
EDISON
MAZDA
M
P
EGYPT

Lamp Seller of Bagdad
1923

ing audience. The demand for books with illustrations, especially those in color, was tremendous. This in turn created a need for good illustrators. Among the artists who emerged to fill this void, Maxfield Parrish undoubtedly stands near the top in the book-illustration field. But Parrish is also known for his long and illustrious career in advertising.

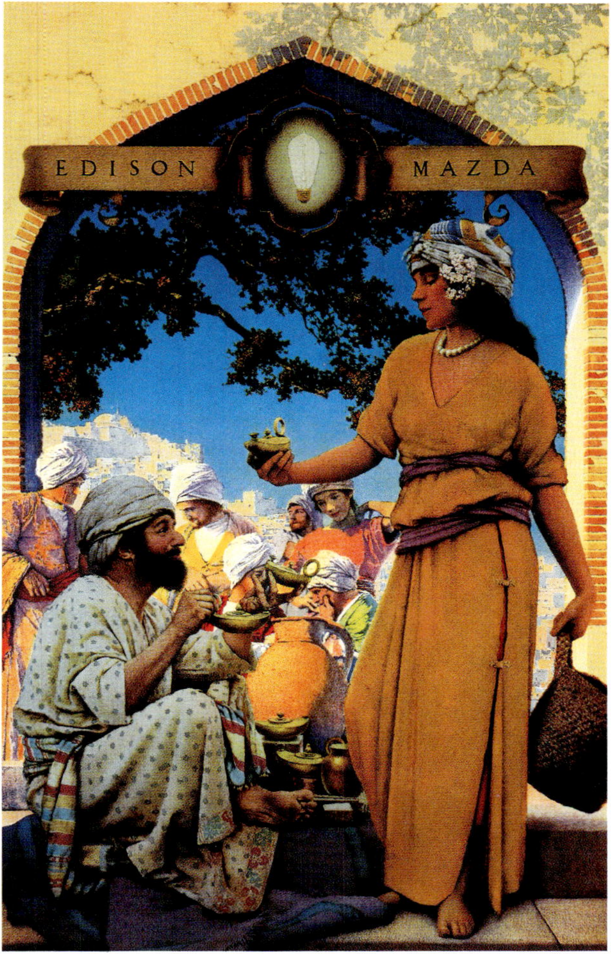
EDISON
MAZDA

Venetian Lamplighter
1924

Though Maxfield Parrish stated he disliked the field of commercial art, he spent most of his career contributing to it. Art critics, who now take Parrish seriously, bemoan Parrish's decision to turn to this art form. Though he eventually fulfilled his dream of being "just a painter," the artist's career was rooted in the commercial field. During his college days,

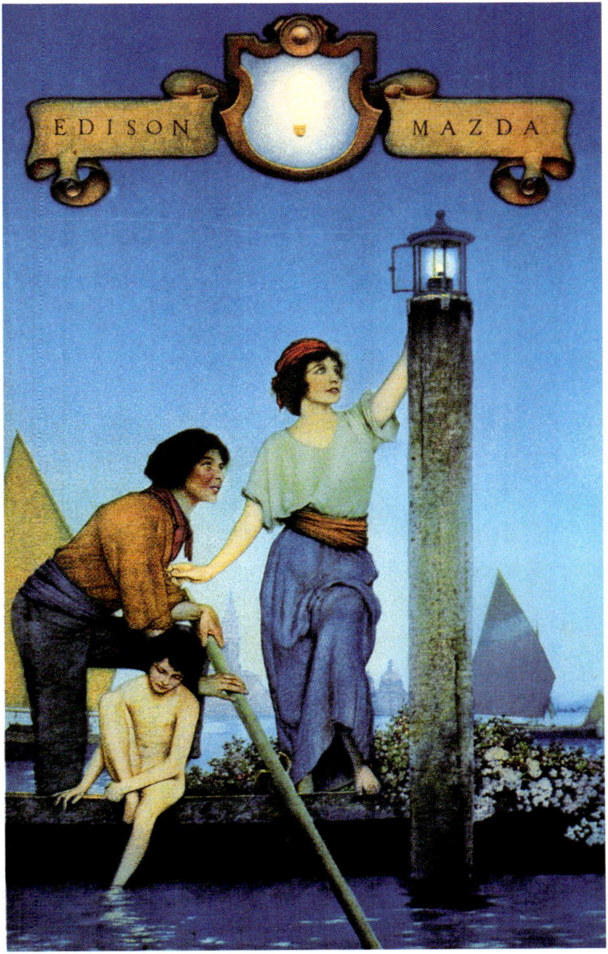
EDISON
MAZDA

Dreamlight
1925

Parrish designed posters, program covers, and flyers for his alma mater, Haverford College, as well as other colleges in the Philadelphia area. His recognition spread, as he won design competitions for posters, advertisements, and magazine illustrations. By the late 1890s, Parrish's work was gaining prominence in other areas of commercial art. His book illustrations

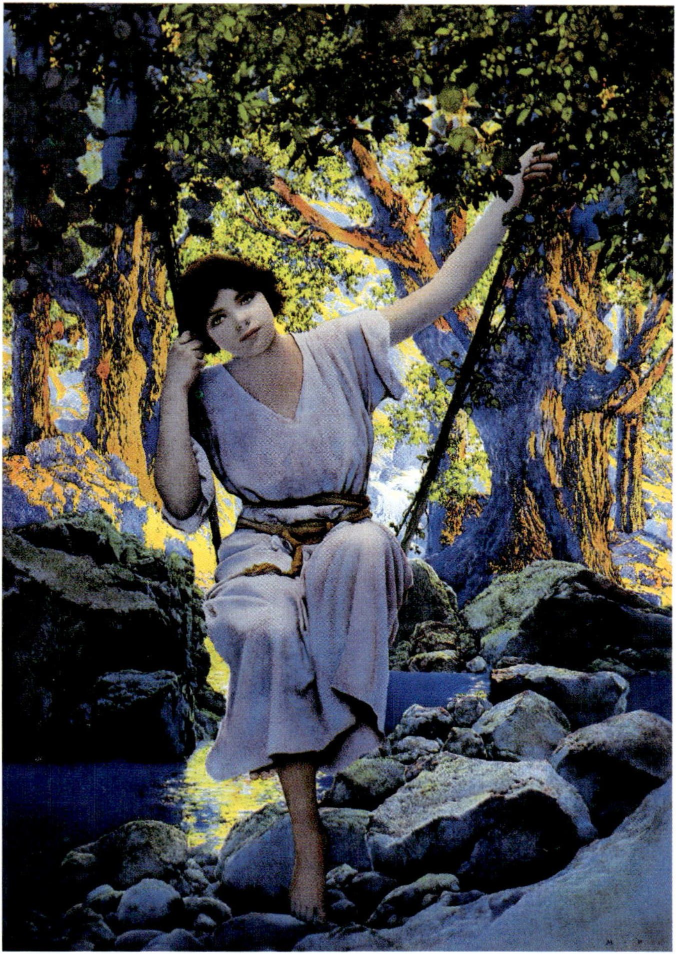

Enchantment
1926

and magazine covers (most notably, *Century Magazine*) were causing a sensation and demand for his work was increasing.

Parrish's early style is more graphic than his later. Earlier works are executed in a two-dimensional style using flat areas of dark contrasted with light, heavier lines and little or no rendering on subjects. Parrish, Will

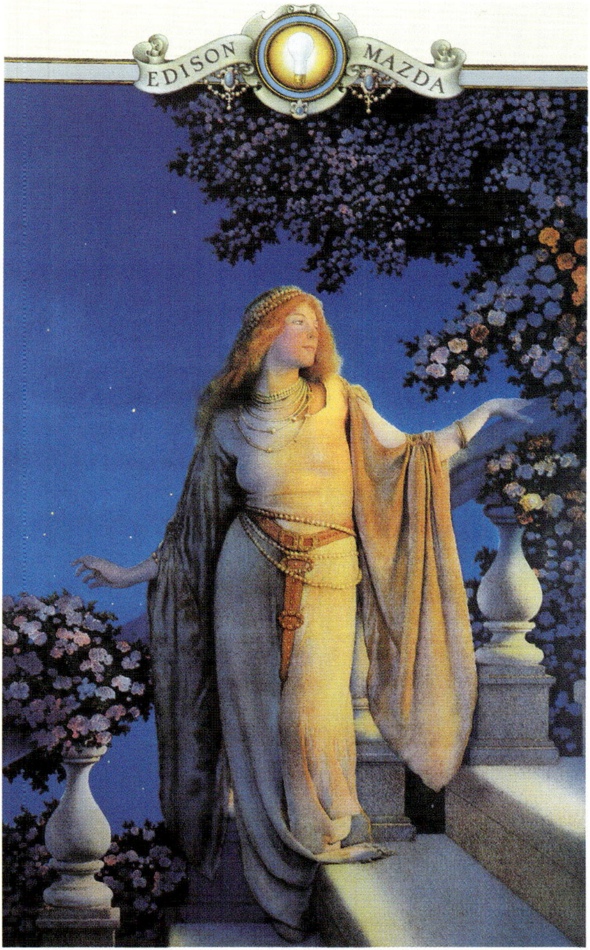
EDISON
MAZDA

Bradley, Louis Rhead, and other graphic artists of the time worked in a style you could call an Americanized Art Nouveau. Art Nouveau, full of curves, flowers, and fantasy, arrived in America just as it was fading in Europe. The Art Nouveau style intensely reflected Japanese design, and these influences appear in Parrish's early designs, as well as those

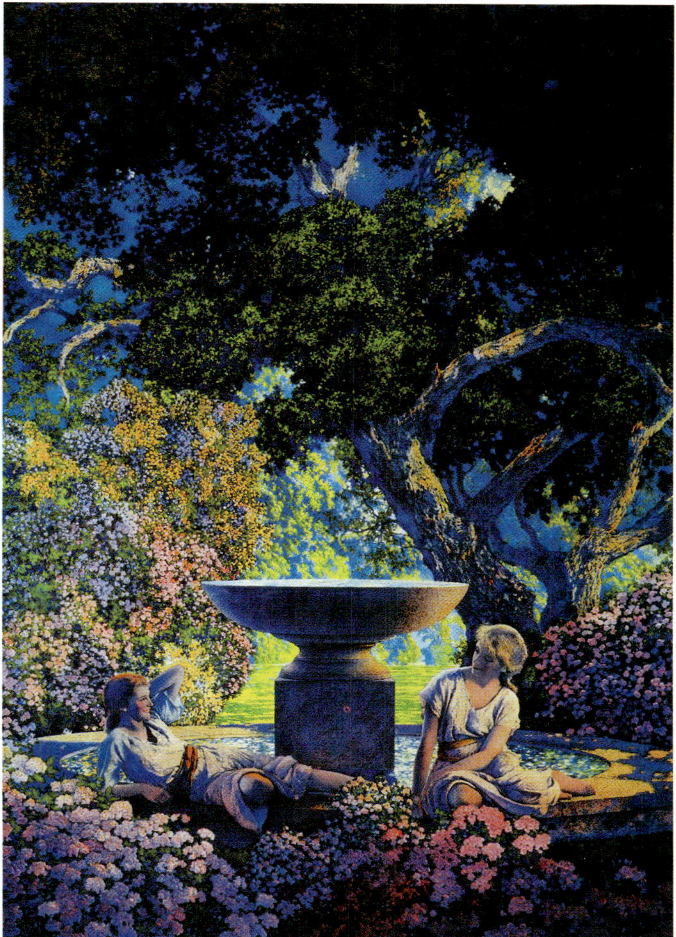

Contentment
1928

of many of his contemporaries. Art Nouveau's more generic influences can also be identified in Parrish's early pieces – the use of legendary figures and the graphically flowing clothing, scrolls, and borders which can be found in many of these designs.

By the early 1900s, Maxfield Parrish had the luxury of turning his back on advertising and spending the

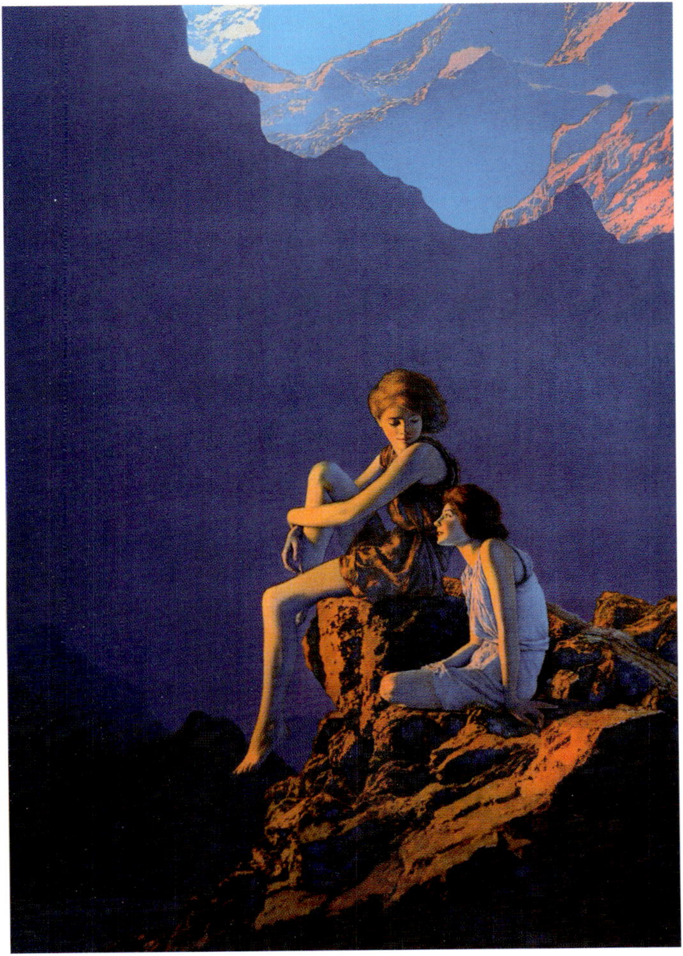

Golden Hours
1929

next decade working solely on book and magazine illustration and mural design. By the mid-teens, Parrish again was contributing to advertising – a move that would eventually lead to his enormous popularity in other fields.

His first new advertising commission was for Crane's Chocolates. Because of this, Parrish became famous for art prints reproduced from

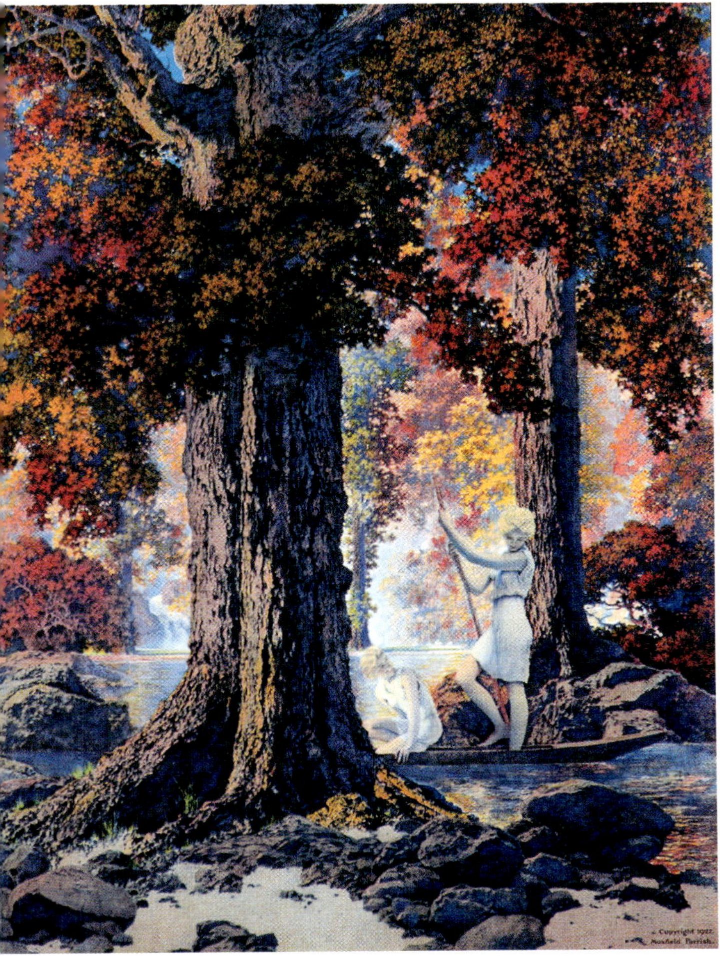
Copyright
Maxfield Parrish

Ecstasy
1930

the advertisements. His next commission for Djer-Kiss Cosmetics resulted in two ads. One depicts Parrish's ethereal maiden amid a profusion of flowers. The second depicts a similar maiden with three elves set on a craggy, wooded hillside. Once his work reappeared in print, Parrish was flooded with offers for jobs. He had the good fortune to turn to Rusling

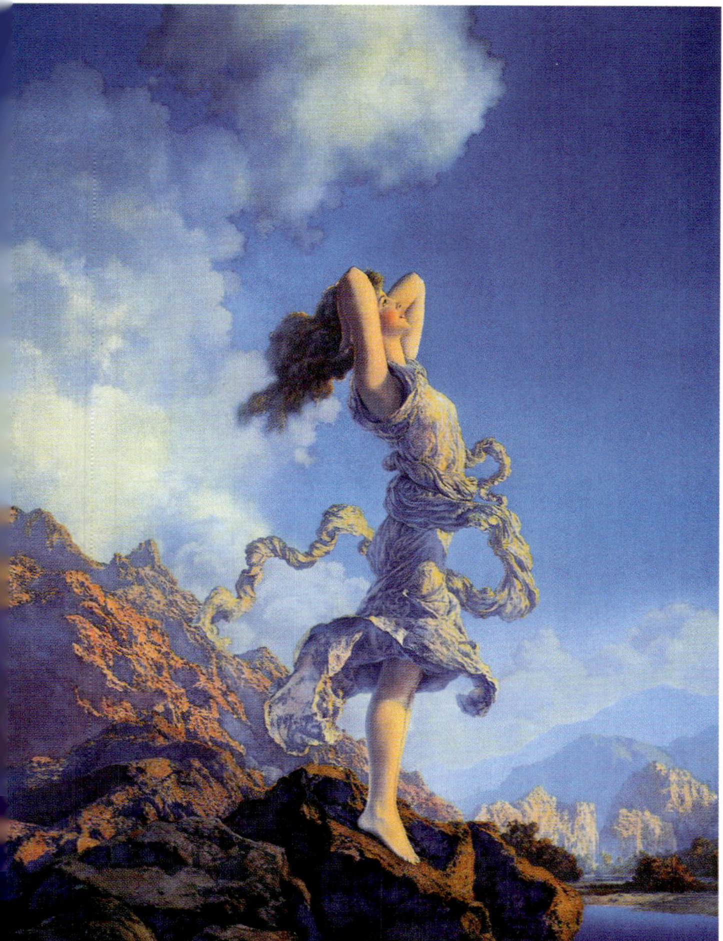

Wood, the owner of a lithography business and an advertising firm in New York. Parrish and Wood entered into an exclusive arrangement, giving Parrish the opportunity to choose which jobs he wanted.

Parrish's contractual agreement was the harbinger of numerous advertising commissions and brought his work to an even wider audience than

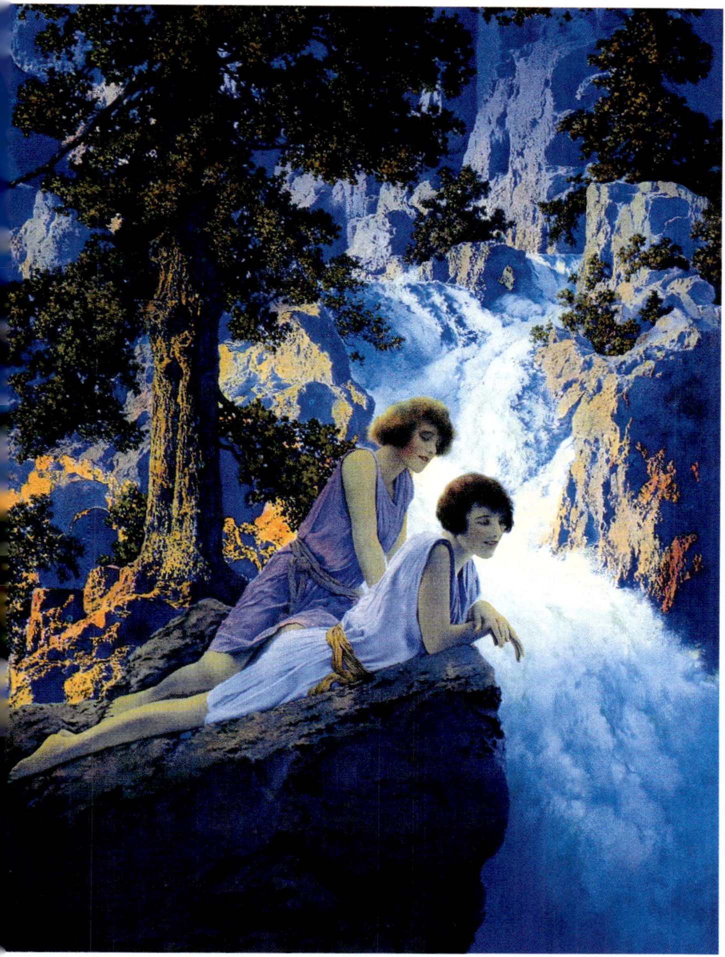

Solitude
1932

did his book and magazine illustrations. (Parrish's career as a book illustrator slowly waned as the sales of his advertising work and art prints escalated.) Parrish's style blossomed with his return to commercial art. Working in full color, he brought to development his trademark photo-realistic landscapes and use of symmetrical figures or objects. Possibly inspired by

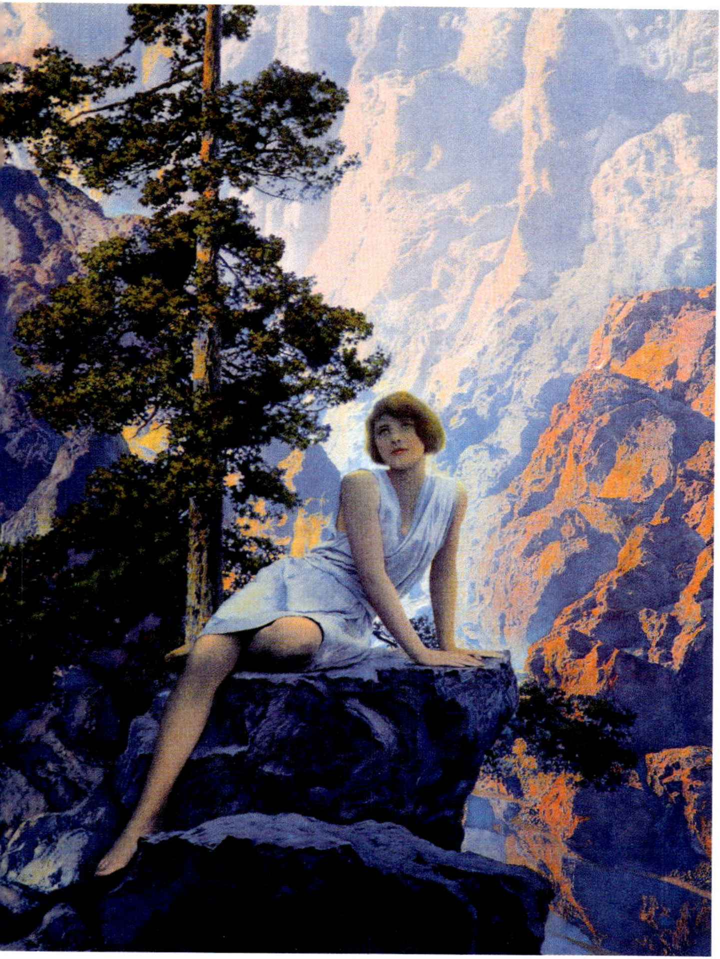

his career as a book illustrator, Parrish employed Mother Goose and fairy-tale characters in most of his advertising art. This imagery was a change from the Djer-Kiss ads, which featured the more familiar maiden in a landscape.

During the artist's association with his printer, he created many well-loved images. Four designs were produced for Fisk Tires – one of Mother

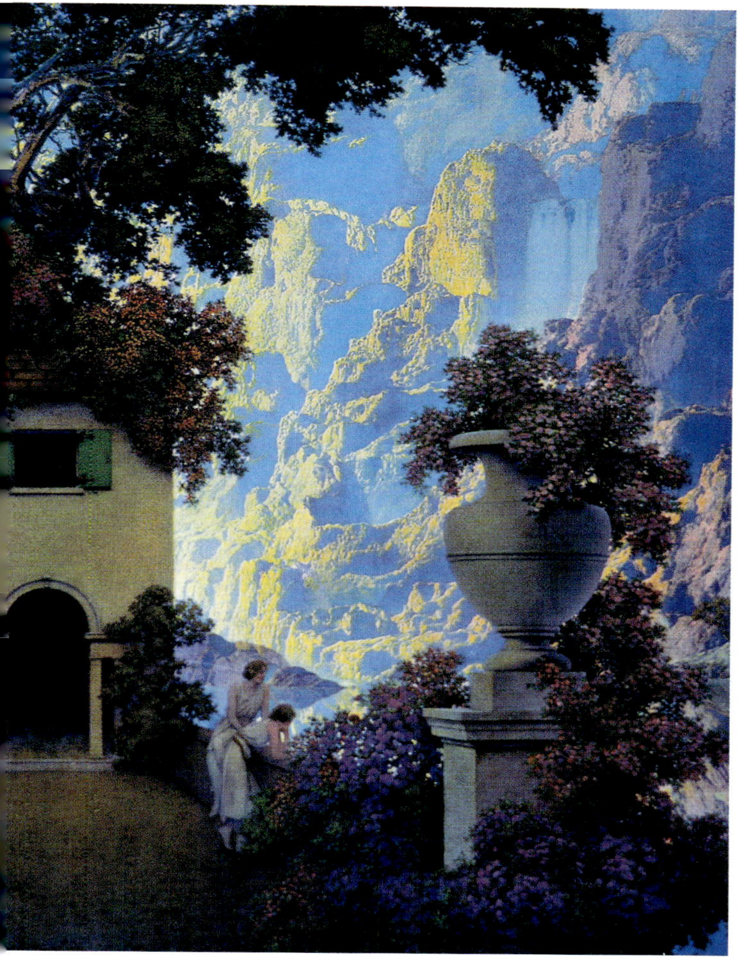

Moonlight
1934

Goose (encircled by a tire) has become well known. Four other designs for the Ferry Seed Company depict the popular characters of Peter, Peter, Pumpkin Eater; Peter Piper; Mary, Mary Quite Contrary; and Jack and the Beanstalk. Other commissions obtained through Rusling Wood include two servants holding a silver chest for Community Silver Company and a beautifully

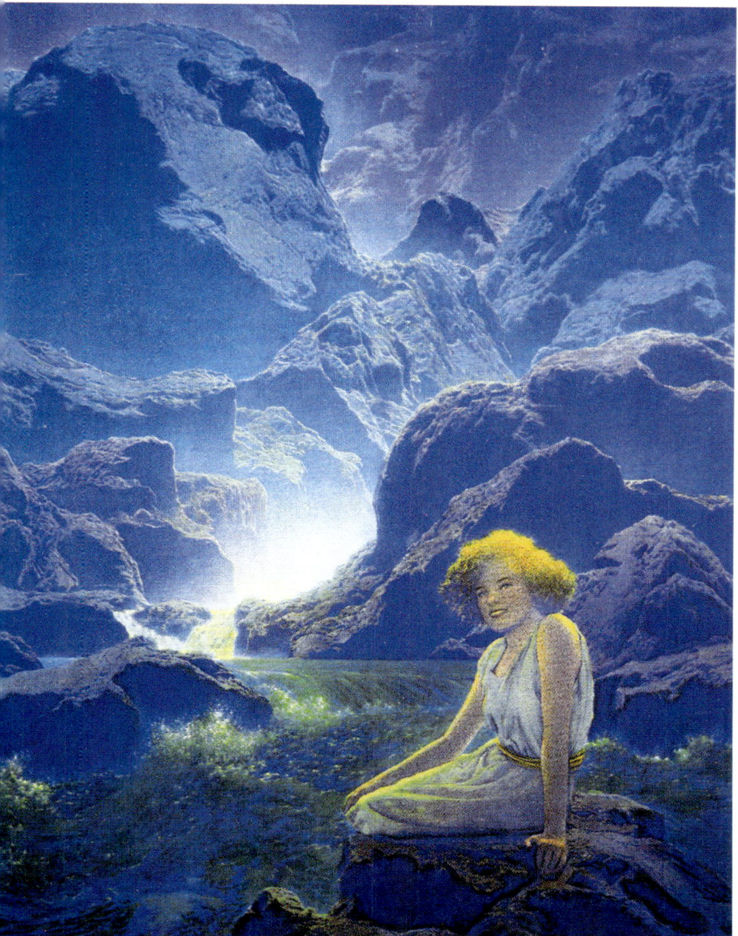

Jell-O "Polly Put the Kettle On"
1922

moody landscape featuring two gnomes brewing Hires Root Beer. Mother Goose characters continue to abound in the advertisement for Swift's Ham (Jack Sprat and his wife) and for Jell-O (Polly Put the Kettle On). The Mother Goose imagery in these advertisements give them an innocent and "sweet" look.

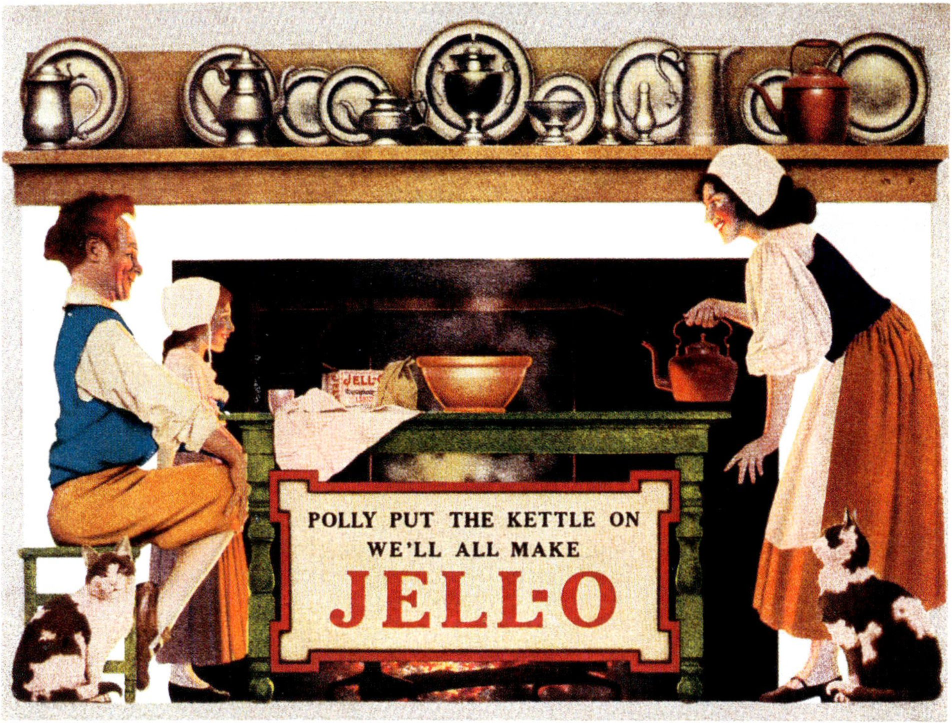
POLLY PUT THE KETTLE ON
WE'LL ALL MAKE
JELL-O

Community Plate
1918

Less charming but no less enchanting was the one other commission Parrish had accepted upon the return to the advertising field. These images, along with his burgeoning art prints, made Maxfield Parrish a household name. After Parrish returned to advertising art in 1915, he was approached by a lithography firm who printed calendars for the Edison

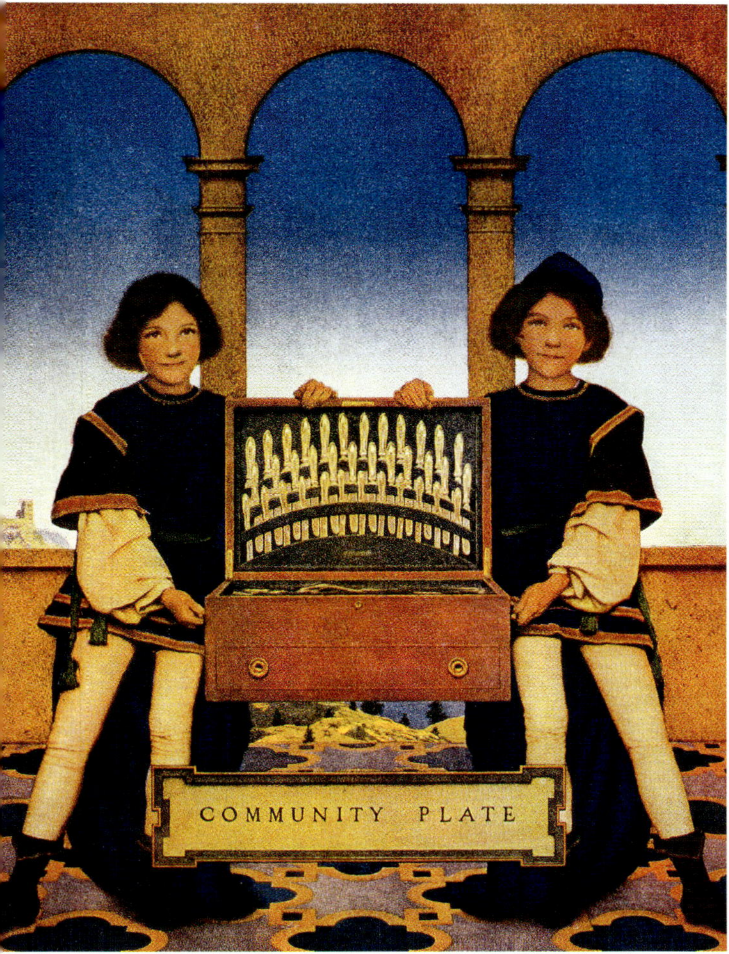
COMMUNITY PLATE

Swift's Premium Ham
1921

Mazda Lamp Division of General Electric. Electric lights were becoming more commonplace in the American home and GE spared no effort or cost in promoting its products. Parrish agreed to do a calendar for the company. His design for the 1918 calendar, *Dawn*, was so successful Parrish continued to design calendars for Edison Mazda until the mid-1930s.

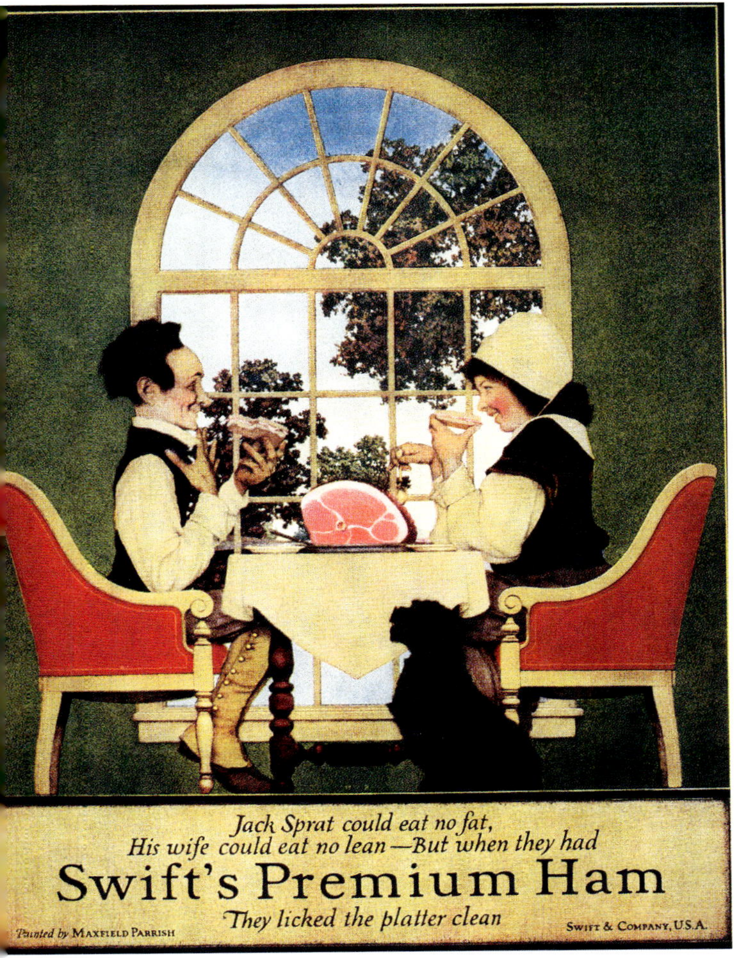

Jack Sprat could eat no fat,
His wife could eat no lean—But when they had
Swift's Premium Ham
They licked the platter clean
Painted by MAXFIELD PARRISH
SWIFT & COMPANY, U.S.A.

Jell-O "King and Queen"
1921

The theme of the early calendars was dictated by GE. The company wanted Parrish to depict the history of light. His nursery rhyme imagery was gone, replaced by allegorical and historical scenes in stunning color and with unique lighting effects. The History of Light series contains the titles *Prometheus, Primitive Man, Egypt, Lamp Seller of Bagdad,* and *Venetian*

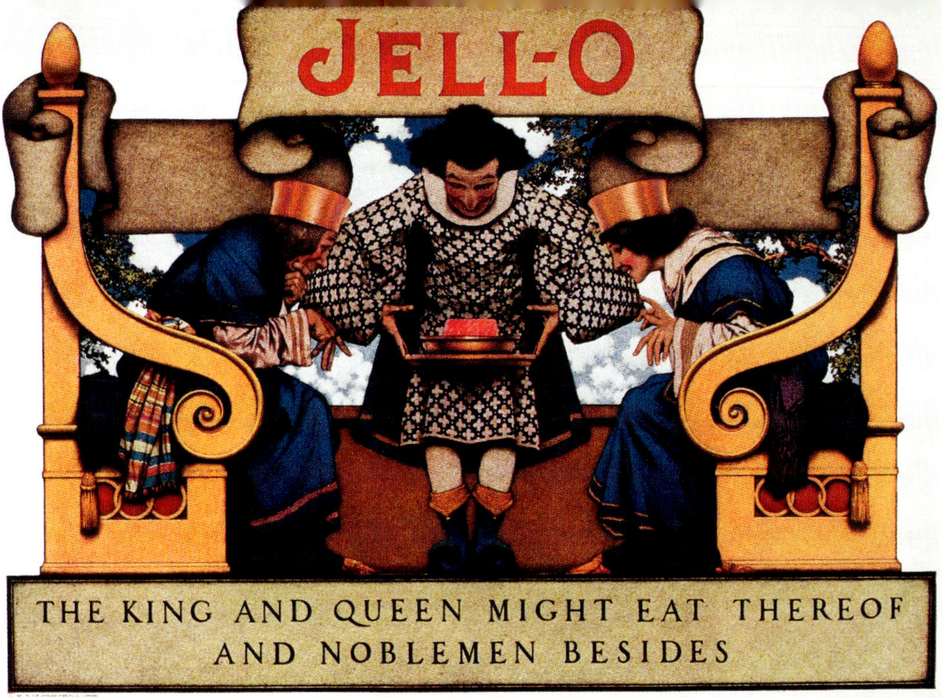
JELL-O
THE KING AND QUEEN MIGHT EAT THEREOF
AND NOBLEMEN BESIDES

Lamplighter. These images are more historical and topical: *Prometheus* delivers light to humankind; in *Primitive Man* firelight is illustrated; and *Egypt* depicts natural light at twilight. The most well known of the series, *Lamp Seller of Bagdad,* is also the most beautifully painted of the early series. The use of shadowed fore-figures and brightly lit backgrounds was

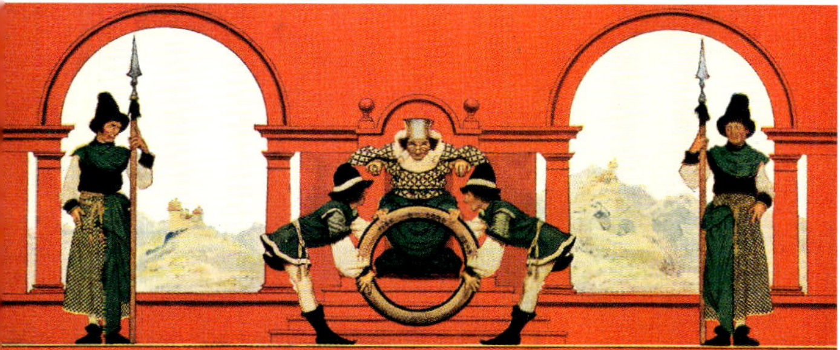

FISK TIRES

"Fit for a King"

REPRODUCTION *of* THE FAMOUS PAINTING MADE *by* MAXFIELD PARRISH *for* THE FISK RUBBER COMPANY

FISK CORD TIRES are made especially for the car owner who can be satisfied with only the highest type of tire construction and quality.

The Fisk Cord is a big tire. It enhances the appearance of a car. It has all the endurance, resiliency, speed, safety, comfort, economy and luxury that can be built into a tire. It is the master work of a great manufacturing institution, whose reputation for many years has been for quality and proven value.

Made with both Ribbed and Fisk Non-Skid Treads

Fisk Tires "Mother Goose"
1919

also employed in the 1925 calendar, *Venetian Lamplighter*. At this point Parrish agreed to continue producing calendar art for Edison Mazda with the stipulation that he dictate the subject and retain control of the artwork (GE had earlier purchased the artwork outright). GE was willing to make any arrangement to keep Parrish, whose calendars had become

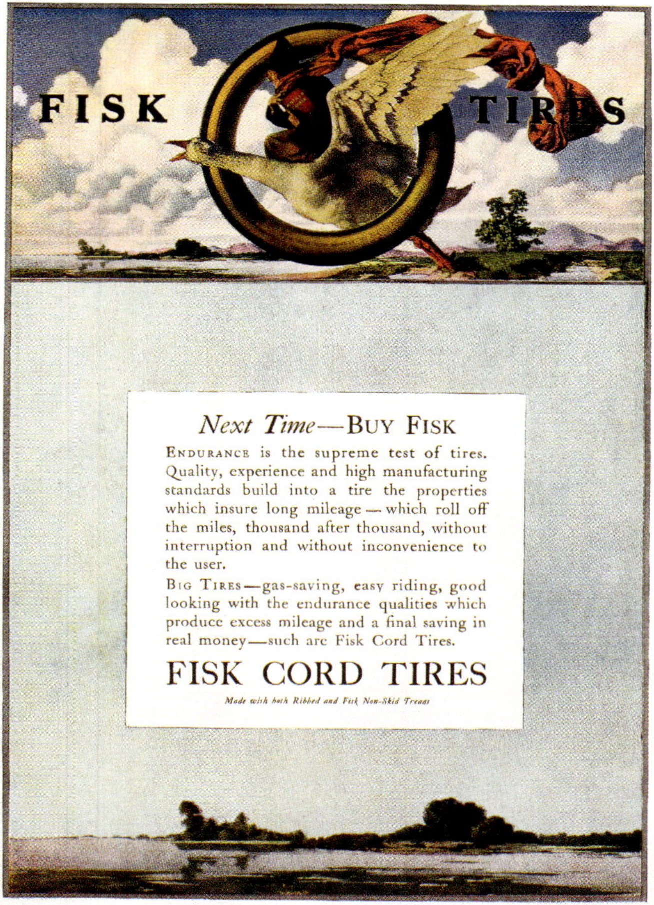
FISK TIRES
Next Time—BUY FISK
ENDURANCE is the supreme test of tires. Quality, experience and high manufacturing standards build into a tire the properties which insure long mileage — which roll off the miles, thousand after thousand, without interruption and without inconvenience to the user.
BIG TIRES—gas-saving, easy riding, good looking with the endurance qualities which produce excess mileage and a final saving in real money—such are Fisk Cord Tires.
FISK CORD TIRES
Made with both Ribbed and Fisk Non-Skid Treads

Djer-Kiss
1918

an integral part of their marketing program. Thus, Parrish continued creating his calendars, but the subjects changed considerably.

Parrish again utilized his maiden(s) amid landscapes ("girls on rocks," as the artist called them) for the remaining calendars for Edison Mazda. The public not only loved the maidens but the landscapes as well,

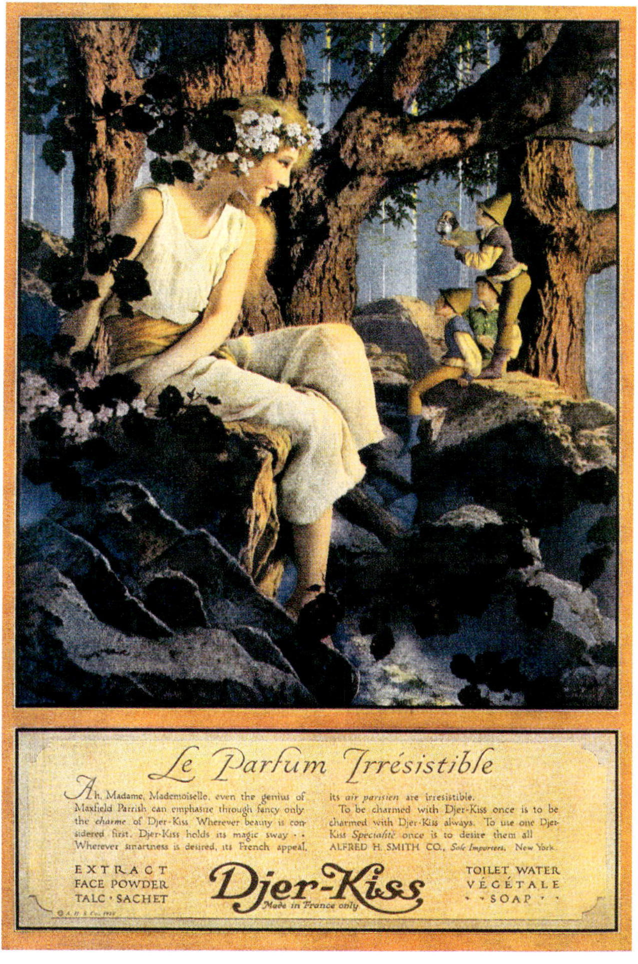
Le Parfum Irrésistible
Ah, Madame, Mademoiselle, even the genius of Maxfield Parrish can emphasize through fancy only the charme of Djer-Kiss Wherever beauty is considered first, Djer-Kiss holds its magic sway · · Wherever smartness is desired, its French appeal, its air parisien are irresistible.
To be charmed with Djer-Kiss once is to be charmed with Djer-Kiss always. To use one Djer-Kiss Specialité once is to desire them all
ALFRED H. SMITH CO., Sole Importers, New York
EXTRACT
FACE POWDER
TALC · SACHET
Djer-Kiss
Made in France only
TOILET WATER
VÉGÉTALE
· · SOAP · ·

Djer-Kiss
1916

which frequently dominated the paintings. The calendars satisfied the artist's desire to paint his landscapes and, at the same time, were a lucrative contribution to advertising art. Owning the artwork gave Parrish the opportunity to reuse them in his burgeoning art-print career. This is not to say the paintings from this series bear a cookie cutter similarity. Some are not as good as others but we still understand that Parrish put his all into each one.

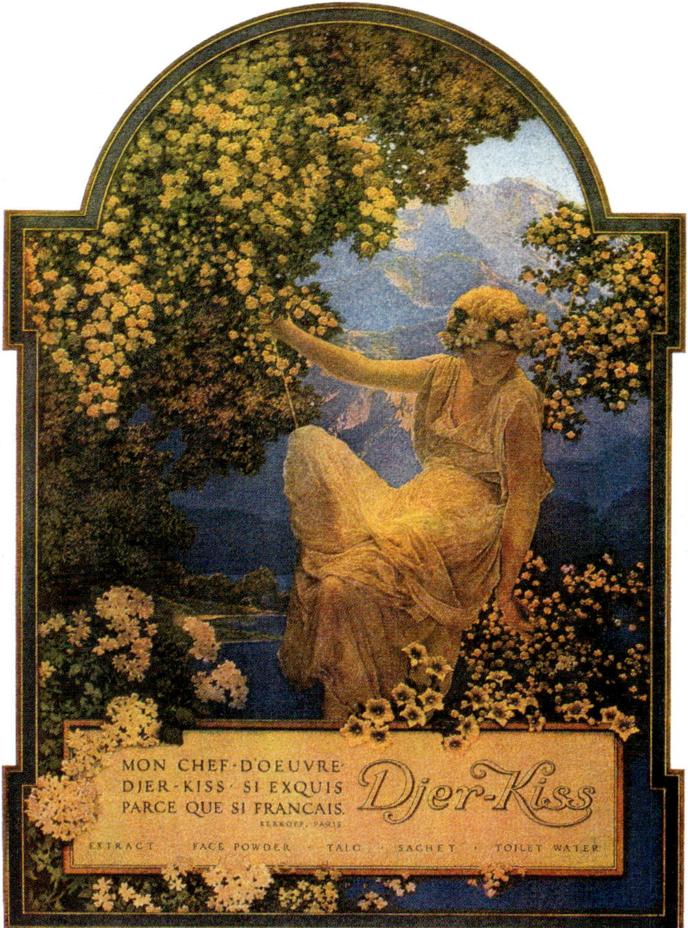
MON CHEF·D'OEUVRE·
DJER-KISS· SI EXQUIS
PARCE QUE SI FRANCAIS.
KERKOFF, PARIS
Djer-Kiss
EXTRACT · FACE POWDER · TALC · SACHET · TOILET WATER

Exhibition of the American Water Color Society
1899

Even with the tight controls Parrish held on the flow of advertising jobs he accepted, he still was not satisfied with the field. By the time he did the Jell-O ads in the early 1920s, the artist was nearing the end of his career in commercial art and was moving on. Parrish was gaining new fame as an art-print and landscape artist, an accomplishment that appealed to him

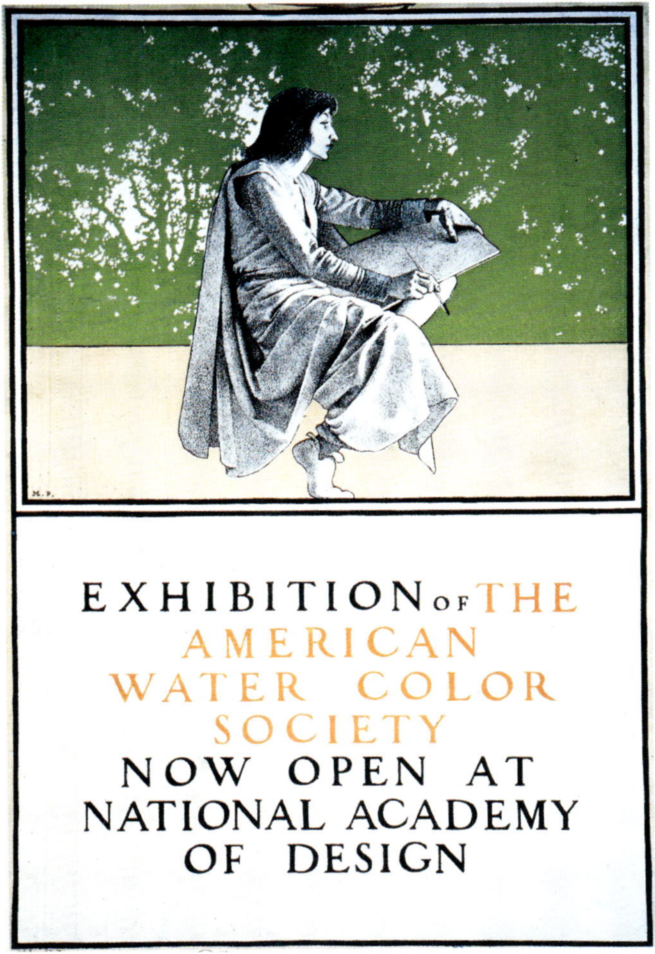
EXHIBITION OF THE
AMERICAN
WATER COLOR
SOCIETY
NOW OPEN AT
NATIONAL ACADEMY
OF DESIGN

Edison Mazda Lamps Logo
1918

greatly. Many of his commercials were being reprinted as art prints – most notably *Garden of Allah* from Crane's chocolate boxes. The originals (on the box) were small and most people did not hesitate spending a quarter for a larger reproduction. The popular response to the Edison Mazda calendars and their reproductions as prints continued to inspire Parrish.

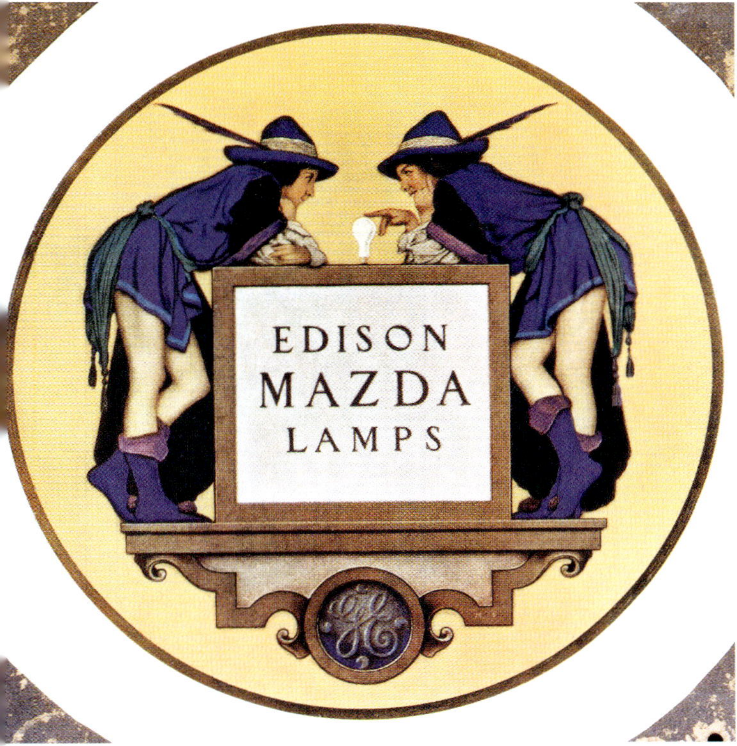
EDISON
MAZDA
LAMPS

Edison Mazda Lamps
1925

By the mid-1930s sales of the Edison Mazda calendars were declining. Parrish saw the need to move on and struck an agreement with the Brown & Bigelow Company to submit a calendar painting each year. Maxfield Parrish went into semi-retirement from advertising art and submitted bucolic landscape paintings to Brown & Bigelow for the rest of his

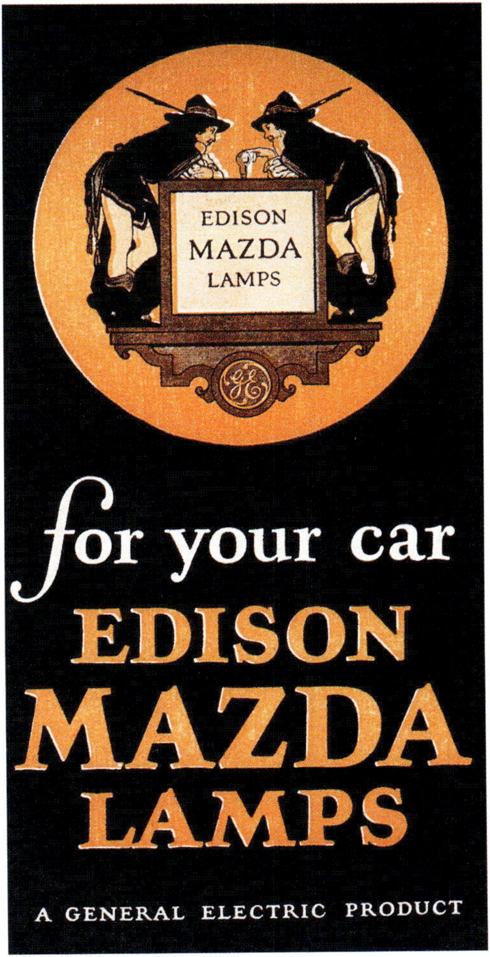
EDISON
MAZDA
LAMPS
for your car
EDISON
MAZDA
LAMPS
A GENERAL ELECTRIC PRODUCT

Ferry's Seeds "Peter, Peter, Pumpkin Eater"
1918

career. Though he maintained he cared little for commercial art, Parrish theoretically remained in the field for his entire life.

So why consider Parrish's commercial work with all those lushly beautiful art prints that the public can't get enough of? Many of the early art prints originally were commercial

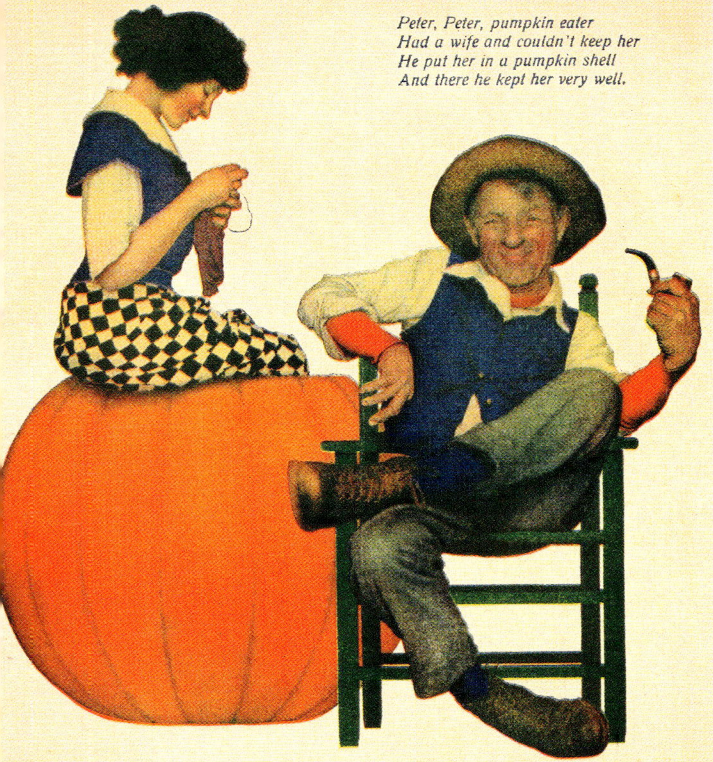

Peter, Peter, pumpkin eater
Had a wife and couldn't keep her
He put her in a pumpkin shell
And there he kept her very well.

This is Peter the Husbander

Peter as a gardener was a failure at first. "A seed's a seed," says he. But his wife left him. Then he got it through his head that the tenderest, most luscious vegetables and the most glorious flowers came from seed taken from the tenderest, most luscious vegetables and the most glorious flowers. You couldn't

Ferry's Seeds "Peter Piper"
1919

projects. As Parrish gained more control over use of his commercial paintings, he was able to utilize them in both fields. By the time he did the Brown & Bigelow calendars, his art was totally divorced from the advertiser or his product. But be it his early works in black and white or later full-color paintings for Edison Mazda, the main reason we appreciate Parrish's work is simply because it's Parrish.

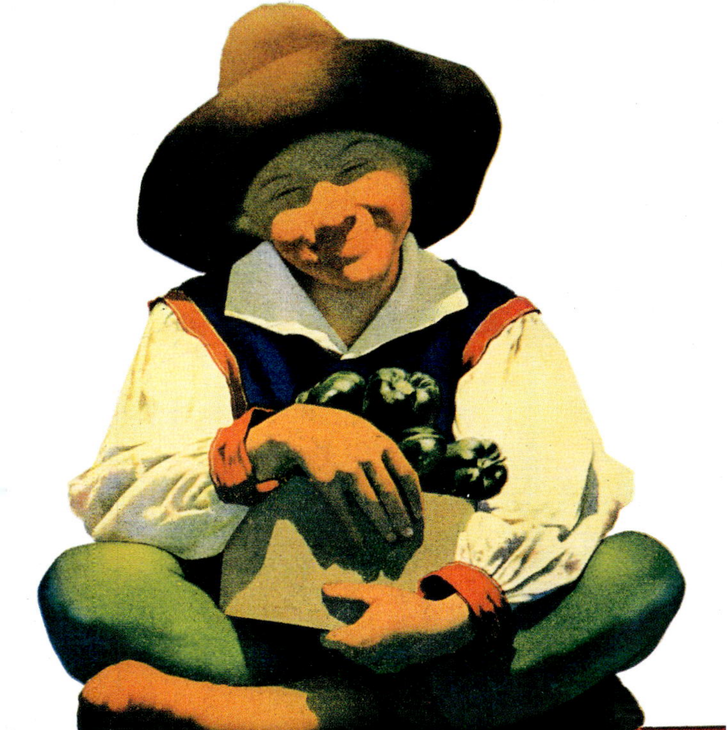

Peter Piper picked a peck of pickled peppers;
A peck of pickled peppers Peter Piper picked;
If Peter Piper picked a peck of pickled peppers,
Where's the peck of pickled peppers Peter Piper picked?

·ETER FIRST PICKED GOOD SEED

Vignettes

Vignettes

Vignettes

Maxfield Parrish

THE MAGAZINE COVERS

Michael J. Goldberg

Collectors Press, Inc.
Portland, Oregon

Acknowledgements

Collection courtesy of Erwin Flacks, Fine Art Marketing Co., and the archives of Collectors Press, Inc.

Editor:
Michael J. Goldberg

Design:
Hoover H.Y. Li

Copyright © 1998 Collectors Press, Inc.

All rights reserved. No part of this book may be reproduced or transmitted in any form or by any means, electronic or mechanical, including photocopying, recording, or by any information storage and retrieval system, without written permission from Collectors Press, Inc.

Published by: Collectors Press, Inc.
P.O. Box 230986, Portland, OR 97281
1-800-423-1848

Printed in Singapore

First American Edition

10 9 8 7 6 5 4 3 2 1

ISBN: 1-888054-22-0

Maxfield Parrish

When illustrator Maxfield Parrish entered the field of magazines and periodicals, he set out to contribute his unique artistic vision to a new medium that was to come into its own.

Magazines and other periodicals had existed since the Colonial days of broadsheets and gazettes. As time went on, the public's interest in printed material grew and flourished so that by the 1890s there was a vast selection from which to choose – from the spicy, pulp-style magazine, *Captain Billy's Whiz Bang,* for those seeking adventure second-hand, to the lavishly illustrated *Studio,* whose pages appealed to intellectuals and artists.

Collier's
May 29, 1909

Somewhere in between lay the great bulk of magazines aimed at the general public; today we might call them "family" magazines. *Harper's*, *Collier's*, *Scribner's*, *Life*, *Ladies' Home Journal*, *Good Housekeeping*, and others made articles and fiction their focal points.

Before radio and television, people cherished books, and reading was a favorite pastime for those of all ages. With the introduction of magazines

June Fiction

Collier's

THE NATIONAL WEEKLY

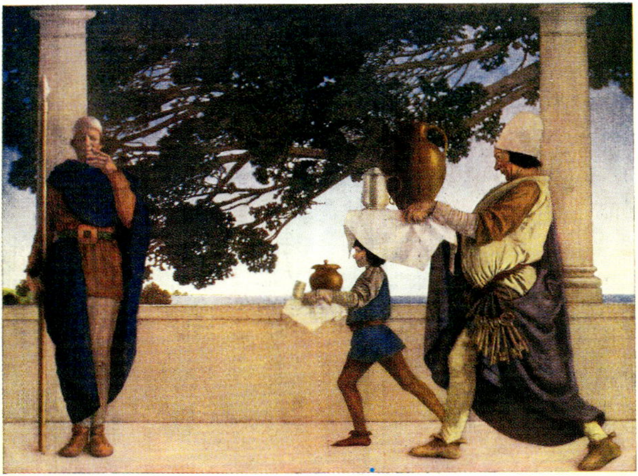

OLD KING COLE

Mural Decoration in the Café of the Hotel Knickerbocker, New York. Painted by Maxfield Parrish

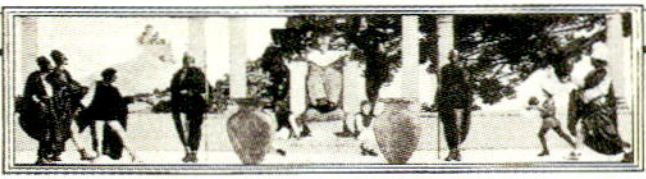

He called for his pipe, and he called for his bowl;

Containing Three Stories:

"WHERE THIEVES BREAK IN"

BY JOSEPHINE DASKAM BACON

THE KING OF COCOANUT ISLAND

BY FREDERICK UPHAM ADAMS

THE THREAD OF GOLD

BY STEPHEN FRENCH WHITMAN

VOL XLIII NO 10 MAY 29 1909

Collier's
June 26, 1909

came a less expensive and more accessible form of written entertainment than books. Well-known authors and poets eagerly contributed to the more popular publications. A writer's subject matter and style not only boosted the magazine's prestige but kept the writer in the public's mind at a time when the only alternative was to read his or her works in the more expensive book format.

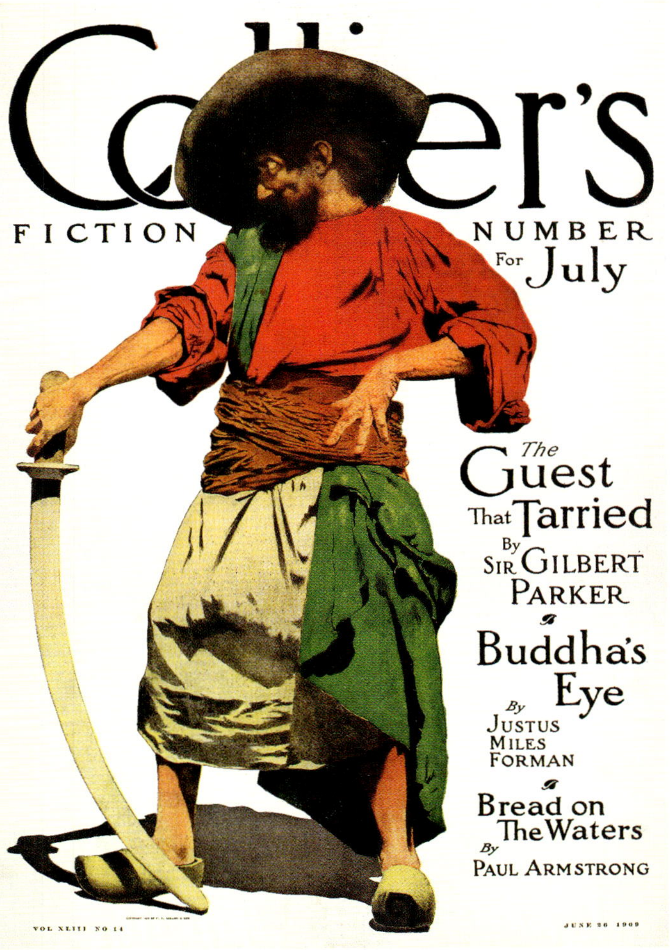

Collier's
FICTION NUMBER
For July
The Guest That Tarried
By Sir Gilbert Parker
Buddha's Eye
By Justus Miles Forman
Bread on The Waters
By Paul Armstrong
VOL XLIII NO 14
JUNE 26 1909

Collier's
October 24, 1936

Many writers gained fame in this period by serializing their novels in magazines. In the early days, magazines also gave fledgling writers a chance to expose their talents in short fiction pieces, articles, or essays. Writing contests, sponsored by the publisher, encouraged both seasoned and amateur authors to submit.

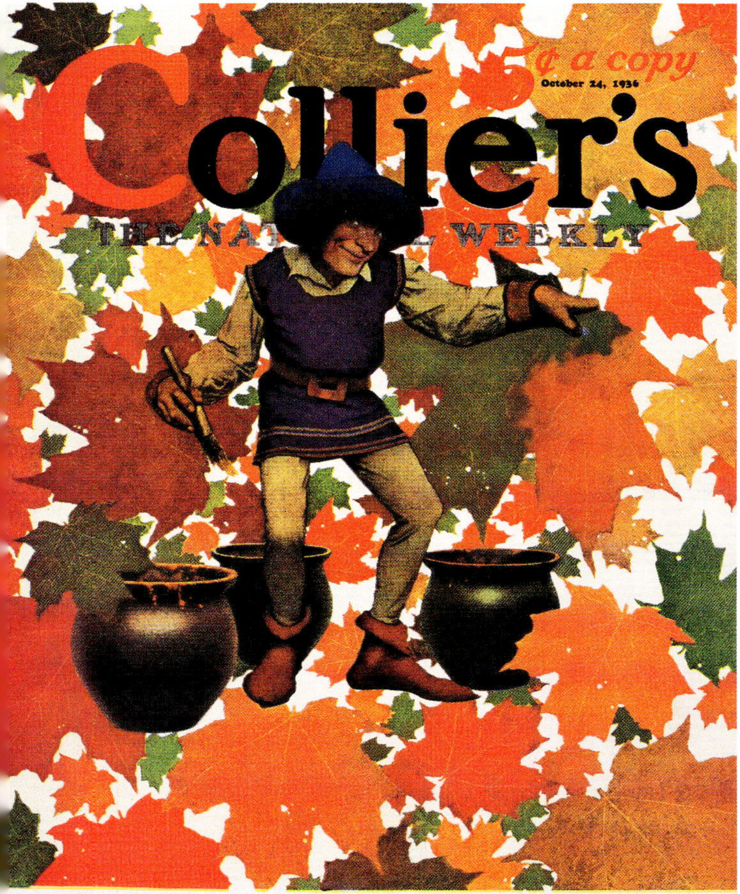

What This Country Needs By John T. Flynn

Collier's
June 6, 1908

A major element of the magazine revolution occurred in the last years of the nineteenth century: artwork on the cover and the inside pages. Printers' ability to reproduce color illustrations increased as photography became an integral part of printing technology. This advance helped create a precise image more efficiently and, in turn, greatly expanded the use of color.

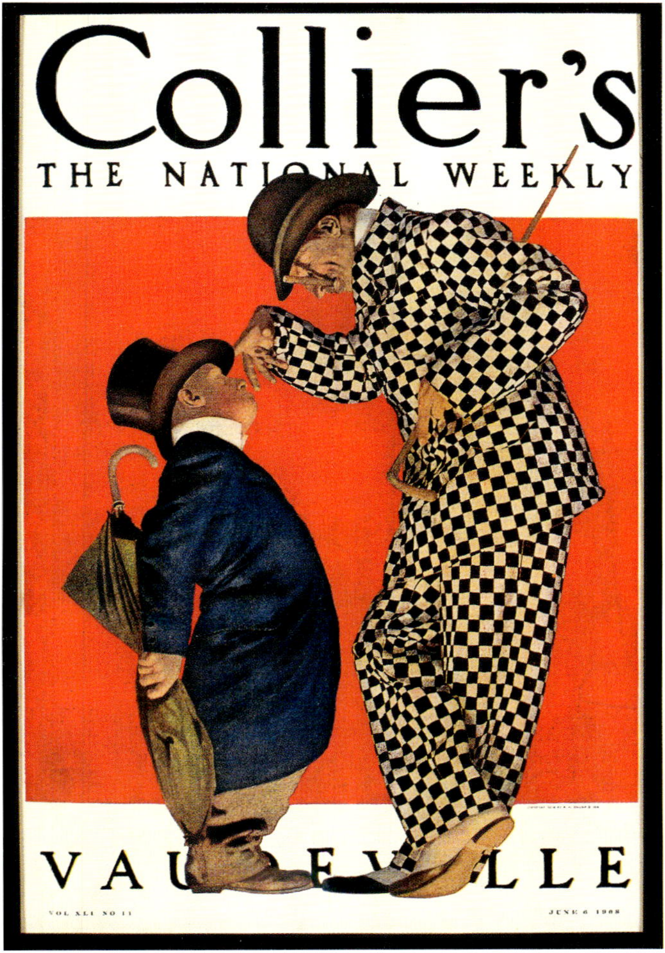
Collier's
THE NATIONAL WEEKLY
VAU E V LLE
VOL XLI NO 11
JUNE 6 1908

Collier's
July 1, 1905

The result was art that caught the attention of the reader, a fact publishers exploited. This was no more evident than in the striking magazine cover designs of the period. Much like their counterparts, widely recognized writers, well-known artists, and illustrators of the time put their hands to supplying stunning black-and-white and color illustrations to the most popular magazines.

Collier's

THE NATIONAL WEEKLY

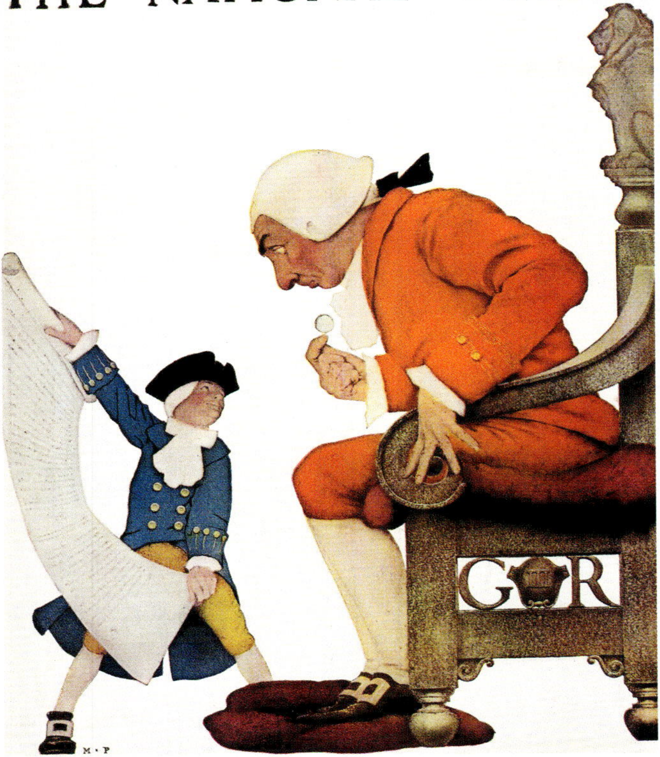

Collier's
June 23, 1906

Maxfield Parrish spent much of his career sporadically contributing to popular publications. As in his art prints and advertising and book commissions, Parrish contemplated and chose works based on their aesthetic appeal to him as well as to the enhancement of his bank account.

Magazine illustration suited him well, as he created a large and fascinating body of work, highlighting different facets of his artistic vision. Parrish

Collier's

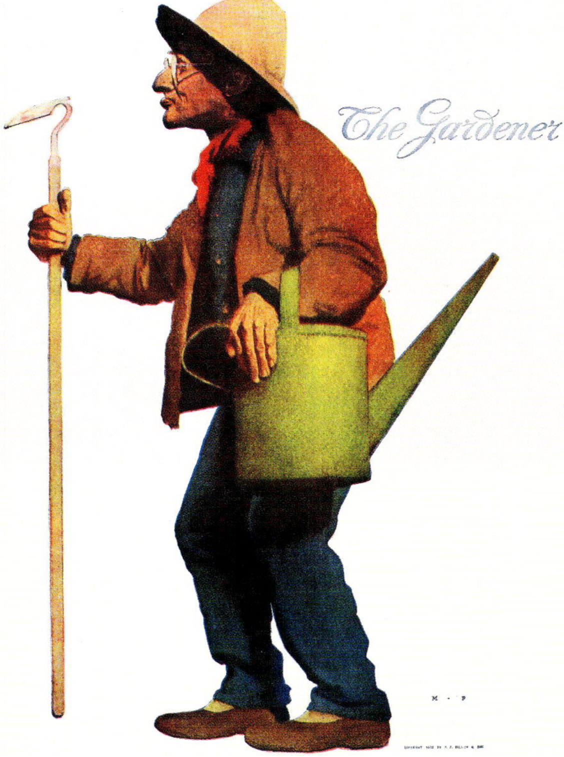

Collier's
July 30, 1910

expanded his scope of subject matter, while retaining some of his stock-in-trade imagery. His magazine work is at once playful, magical, sometimes comical – and always popular. Long before Parrish gained renown for his art prints, people tore his full-page illustrations and covers from magazines for framing.

Parrish began his magazine illustration career when he was approached by Harper and Brothers to submit a

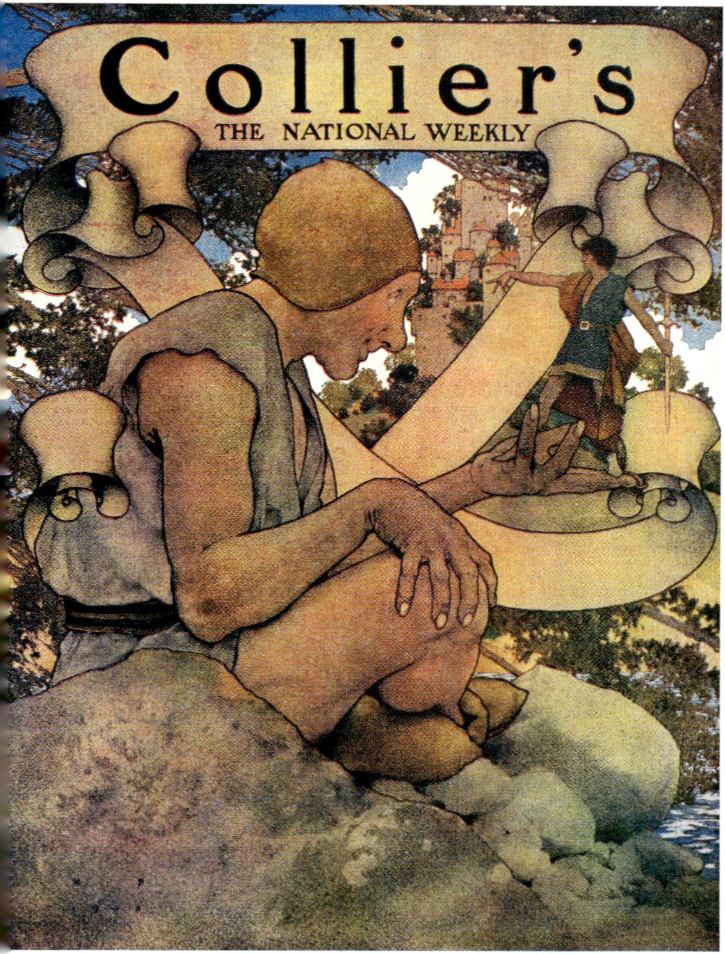
Collier's
THE NATIONAL WEEKLY

Collier's
July 24, 1909

design for *Harper's Bazaar* Easter 1895 issue. Readers enthusiastically accepted his work, and he went on to design covers for other publications by Harper and Brothers including *Harper's Weekly* and *Harper's Young People*.

Within a few years of his arrival on magazine covers, Parrish was asked to design covers for and illustrate *Scribner's Magazine*. The artist's first work for *Scribner's* was a set of drawings for a short story from *Dream Days*

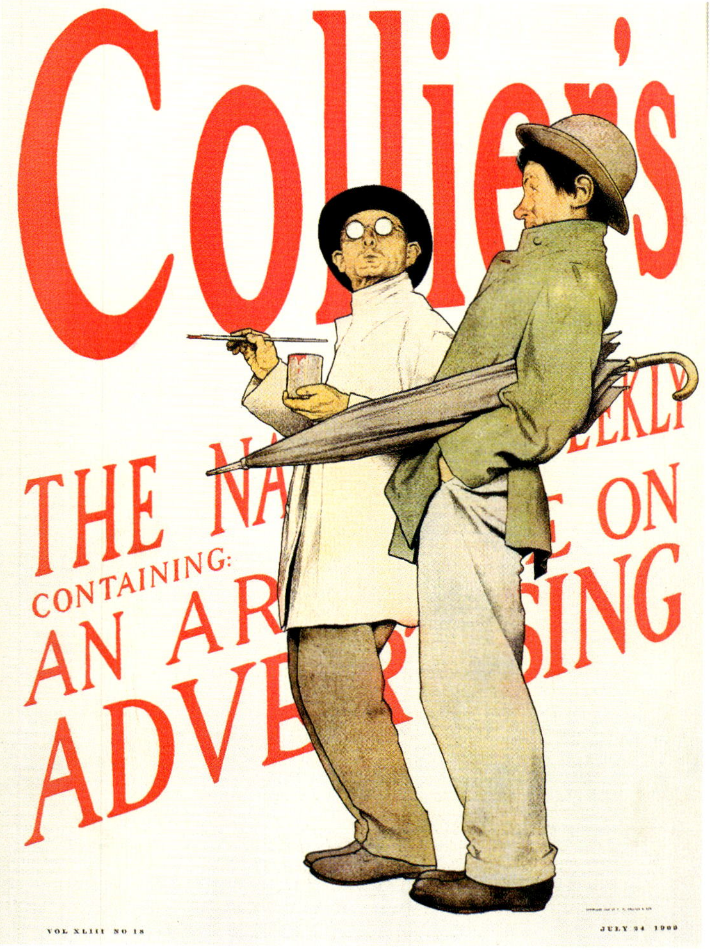
Collier's
CONTAINING:
VOL XLIII NO 18
JULY 24 1909

Scribner's Magazine
April 1899

by Kenneth Grahame. These evocative and charming drawings elicited further requests from *Scribner's*. Parrish responded by submitting more beautiful covers and stunning illustrations to the magazine through the early 1900s.

At the end of the century, Parrish's style shifted towards imagery we identify today as "quintessential Parrish." His earlier style, also evident in his advertising work, is best exemplified by the covers for *Harper's*.

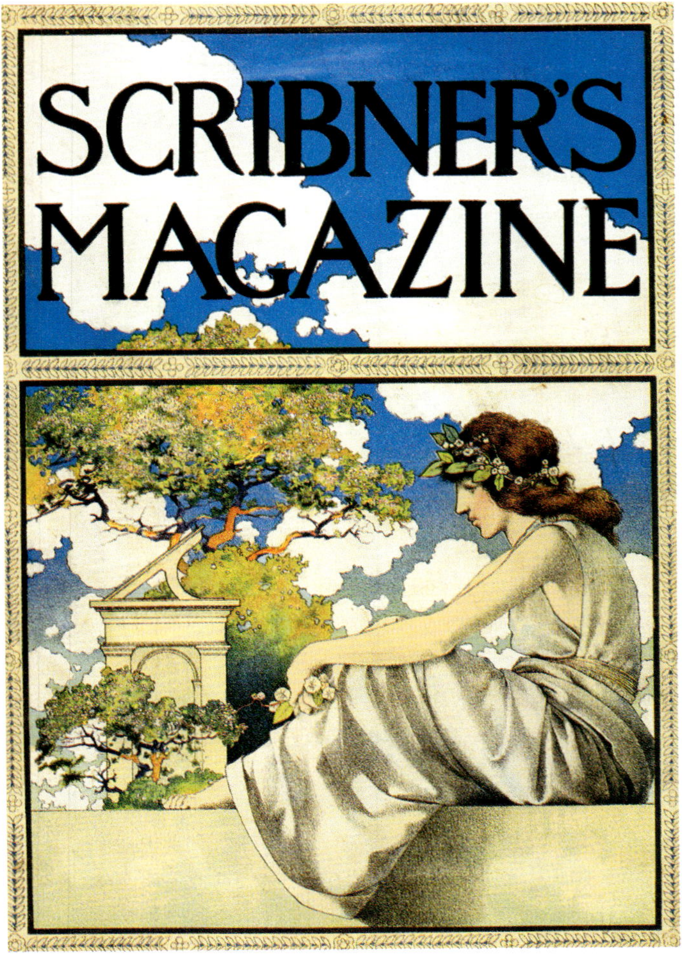
SCRIBNER'S
MAGAZINE

Ladies' Home Journal
June 1914

Working in the "poster style," Parrish drew bold outlines and laid down flat areas of color or patterns, reflecting the essence of the Art Nouveau style.

His first cover for *Harper's*, Easter 1895, combines these influences as well as Art Nouveau's passion for graceful women and stylized flowers. The female figure remained a powerful central figure in Parrish's work as well as that of many of his contemporaries.

THE SUMMER STORY NUMBER

THE LADIES' HOME JOURNAL

JUNE 1914

FIFTEEN CENTS

THE
CURTIS PUBLISHING
COMPANY
PHILADELPHIA

Copyright, 1914 (Trade-Mark Registered), by The Curtis Publishing Company, in the United States and Great Britain. London: 6 Henrietta Street, Covent Garden, W. C.

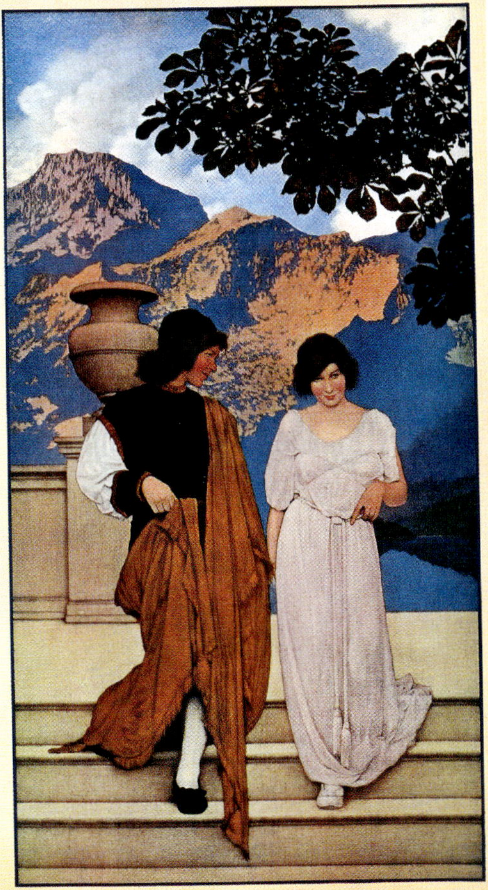

PAINTED BY MAXFIELD PARRISH

Ladies' Home Journal

June 1930

Like illustrators Louis Rhead and Will Bradley, Parrish embraced the works created a few decades earlier by English pre-Raphaelite artists. The women of Parrish's art could be the daughters of Millias', Hunt's, or Rossetti's favorite models.

Parrish's covers for *Scribner's* and other clients, beginning in about 1897, coincided with the fruition of his popular style. The flat poster approach

JUNE, 1930
Volume XLVII, Number 6

10 Cents By subscription $1.00, In the United States and in Canada

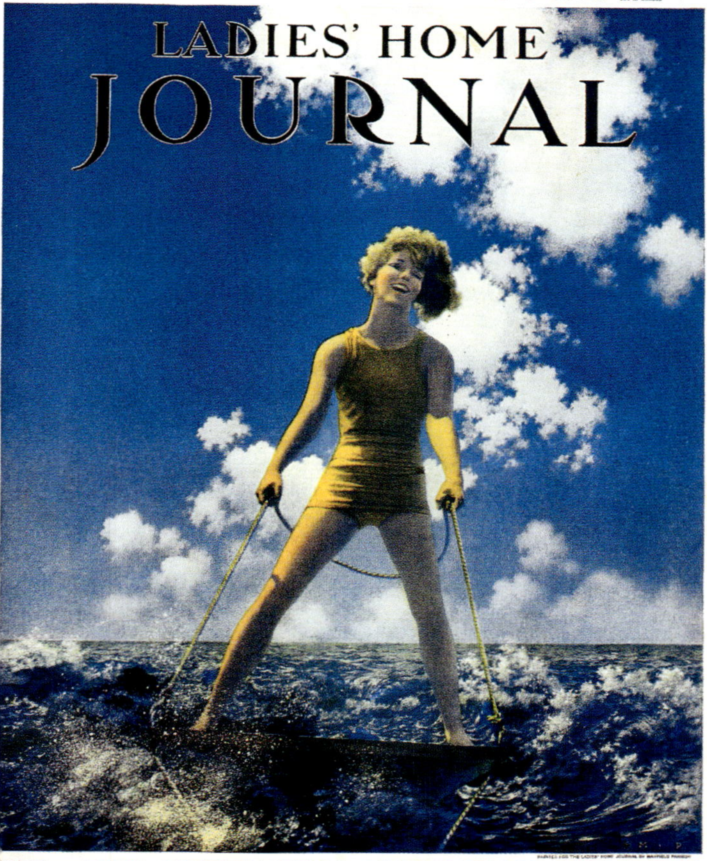

PAUL DE KRUIF—DOROTHY SPEARE—LYNN MONTROSS—MARY GARDEN
SOPHIE KERR—REGINALD WRIGHT KAUFFMAN—DAY EDGAR—JAY GELZER

Life
March 17, 1921

gradually gave way to full color with detail and shadowing to create additional depth. By 1899, *Scribner's* covers were featuring the Parrish maiden reposed in a diaphanous gown. On the April 1899 cover, such a maiden reclines amid flowers and neo-classic architecture. Her Greco-Roman features recall her pre-Raphaelite heritage.

With the October 1899 cover, the same theme is revisited, but the woman has become more Anglicized and closer

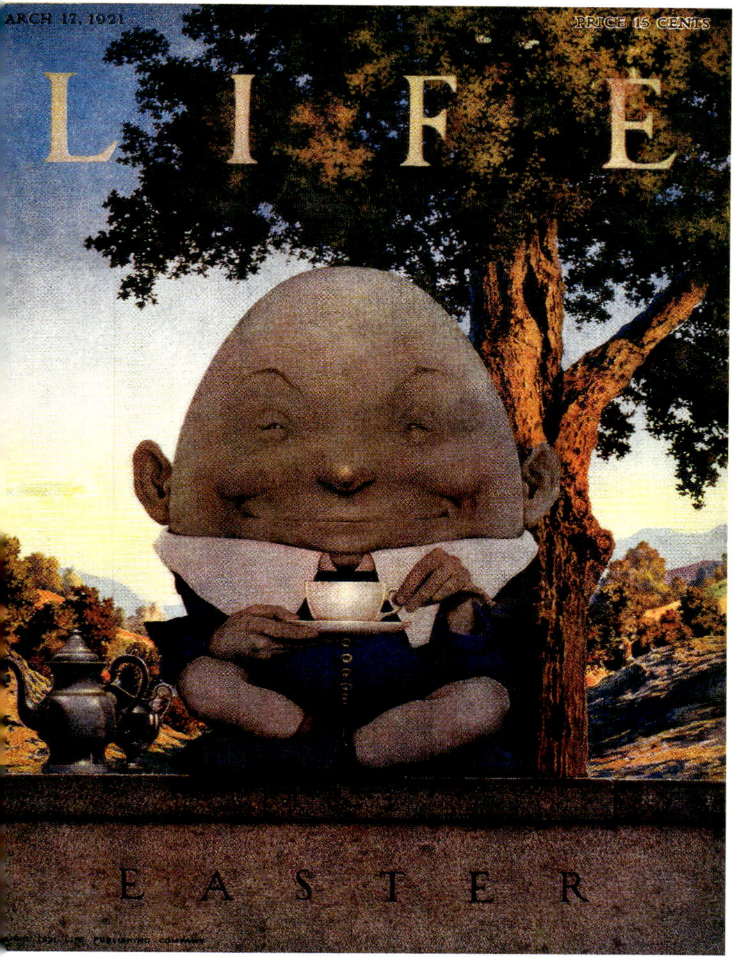
ARCH 17, 1921
PRICE 15 CENTS
LIFE
EASTER

Collier's
January 5, 1907

to the standard Parrish woman usually set within his lush landscapes. The Christmas 1900 cover features a maiden backlit by a full moon. The romantic imagery and lighting effects recall the style of the early "calendar" and print artists also working at this time. Surely they had felt Parrish's influence.

About this time, Parrish received two commissions for the *Ladies' Home Journal* that became milestones in the

Collier's

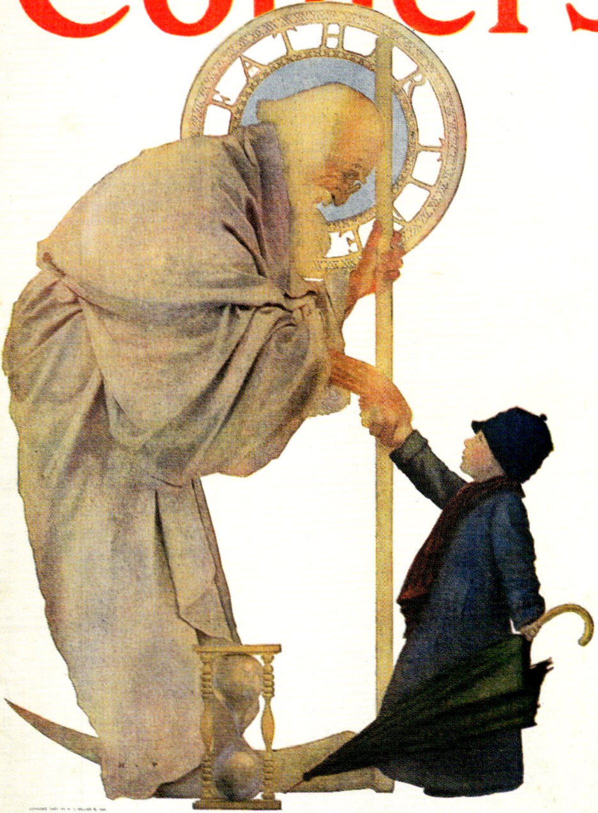

VOL XXXVIII NO 15 JANUARY 5 1907 PRICE 10 CENTS

Life
November 10, 1921

Parrish mythology. He had already completed covers for the magazine when the editors asked him to submit a set of illustrations for poems by Eugene Field. Parrish created five illustrations, all of which were warmly greeted and later assembled in book form.

Even more important in Parrish's career was winning the *Ladies' Home Journal* contest for a cover design. The piece, entitled *Air Castles*, graced the

Life

VEMBER 10, 1921

Volume 78

Copyright, 1921, Life Publishing Company

Number 2036.

PRICE 15 CENT

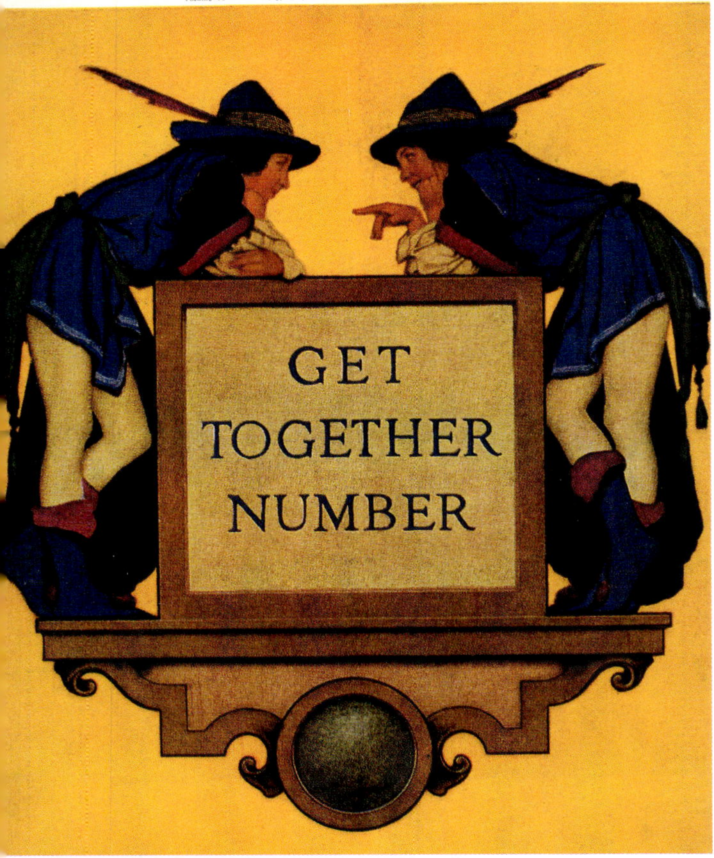

Life
July 20, 1922

cover of the September 1904 issue. It depicts an androgynous youth atop a hill as he blows soap bubbles into a sky resplendent in Parrish blue and accented by tumbling clouds. The piece was so popular that the *Journal* offered reproductions for 25 cents. This marked the beginning of Parrish's career as an art-print artist, although he did not create most of his art-print work until the 1920s.

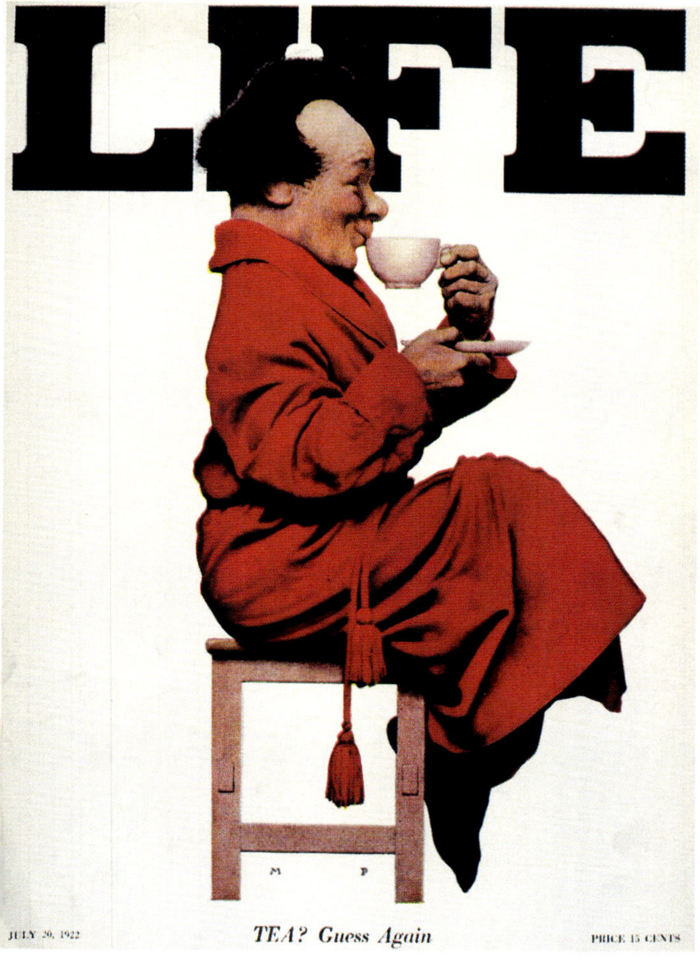
LIFE
JULY 20, 1922
TEA? Guess Again
PRICE 15 CENTS

Life
March 3, 1904

While *Air Castles* was creating such broad excitement, Parrish began work for another magazine that eventually transformed his work, as well as highlighted his now familiar subject matter. In 1904, Parrish signed an exclusive agreement to illustrate for *Collier's* magazine. (*Collier's* paid for the rights to reproduce the artwork while the artist retained ownership of the art,

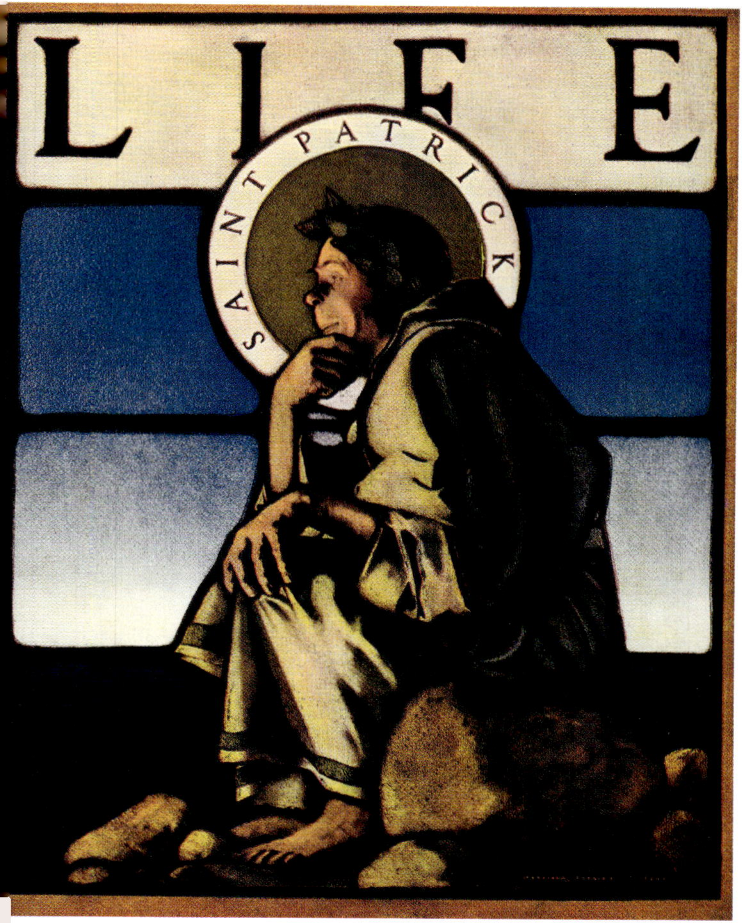
LIFE
SAINT PATRICK

Life
October 19, 1922

an agreement Parrish henceforth included in all his contractual work.)

Parrish's cover designs for *Collier's* appeared between 1904 and 1913. Viewed as a whole, the illustrations display an enormous diversity within the Parrish pantheon. *Collier's* represents Parrish's longest tenure with a single magazine. Consequently, this large body of consistent work

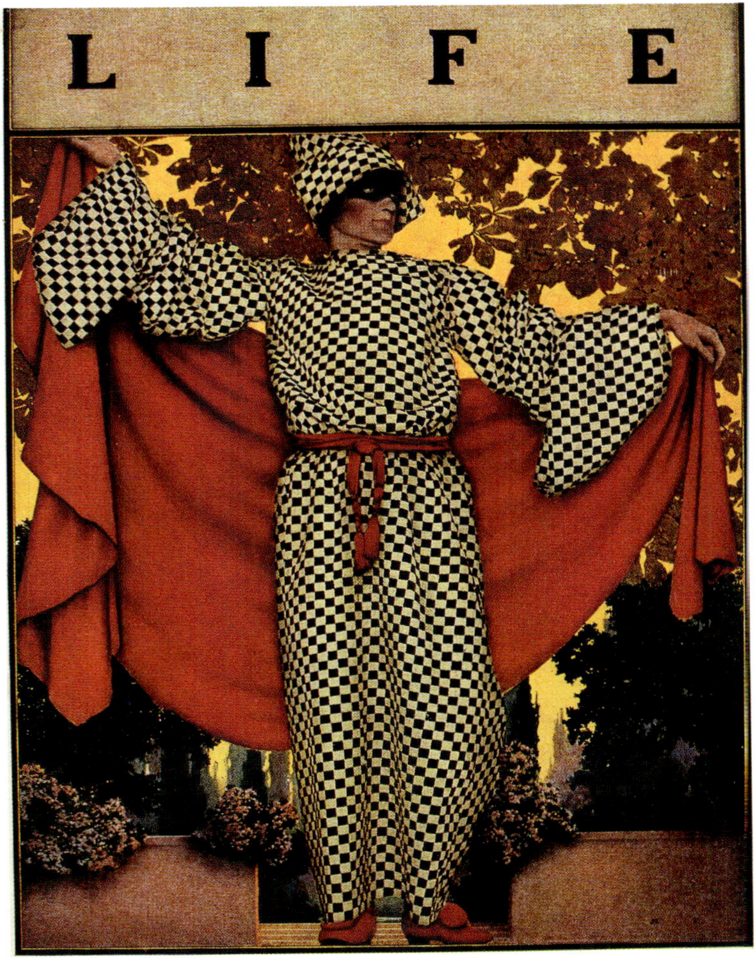
LIFE

Life
June 22, 1922

comprises some of Parrish's best-conceived designs for magazine covers. Not only did he portray the ethereal maids and make-believe characters, but he also conceived numerous covers using average people in poignant and comical situations.

Like his fellow magazine cover artists J. C. Leyendecker and Norman Rockwell, Parrish set average individu-

$800.00 in Prizes for the Best Titles

See Page 10

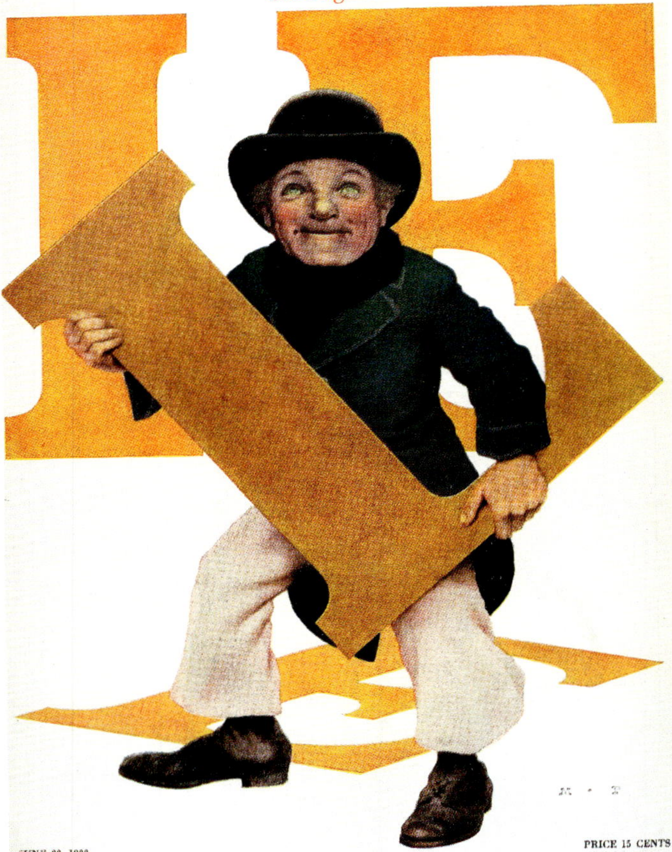

JUNE 22, 1922

PRICE 15 CENTS

Life
March 1, 1923

als in situational backgrounds. (Rockwell went on to pre-eminence in this genre.) These include the Thanksgiving 1905 cover depicting a tramp; *Harvest*, September 1905, showing a farmer with a plow set against a glowing orange sky; and "Independence Number," July 1906, featuring marching, flag-carrying children.

LIFE

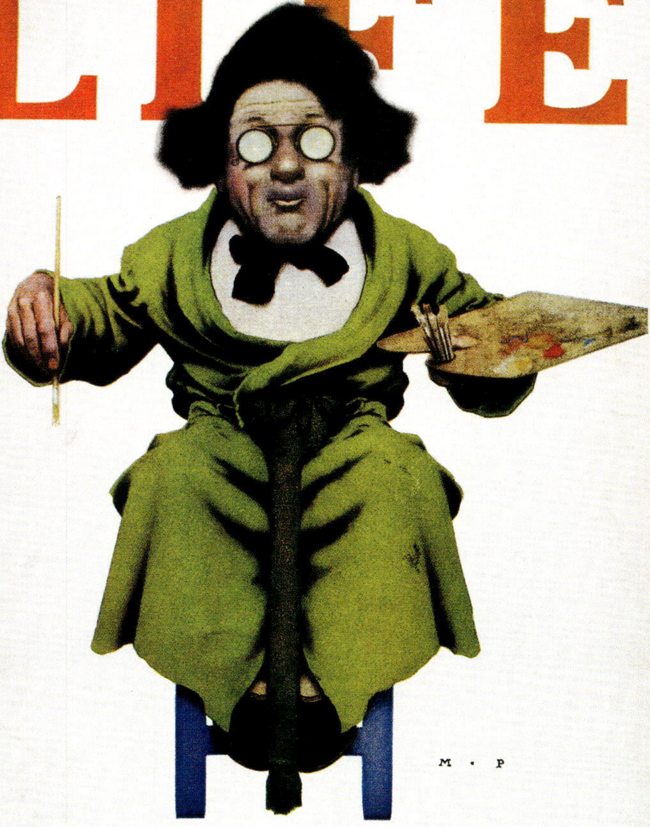

ARCH 1, 1923

A Dark Futurist

Painted for Life by Maxfield Parrish

PRICE 15 CENTS

Life
May 11, 1922

Human beings, allegorical and real, populate many of Parrish's seasonal and holiday covers. Typical Parrish are the covers for Easter 1905; Spring, May 6, 1905; and Christmas 1909. Parrish also incorporated common men and women on his covers, but using a new visual twist, a gimmick he later used in his work for *Life*.

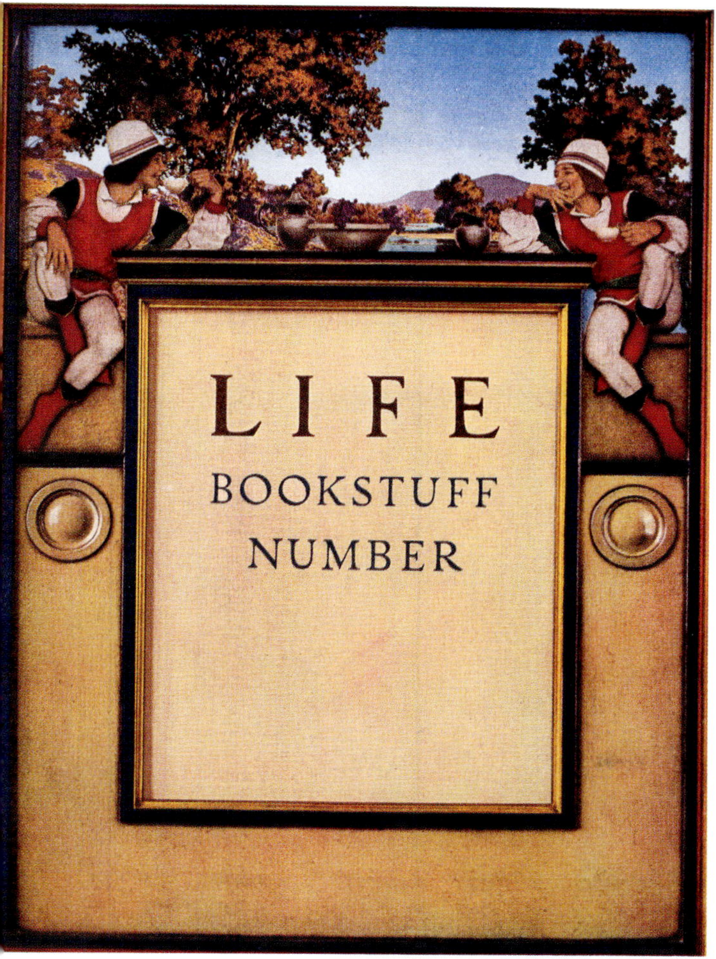
LIFE
BOOKSTUFF
NUMBER

Life
December 7, 1922

Instead of his lush landscapes, Parrish posed his figure(s) against a stark background or solid white field. This seemed so un-Parrish, but the technique gave the artist a break from painting landscapes and offered a chance to focus on using the figure(s) as a graphic element.

The January 5, 1907, cover depicts Father Time greeting the baby

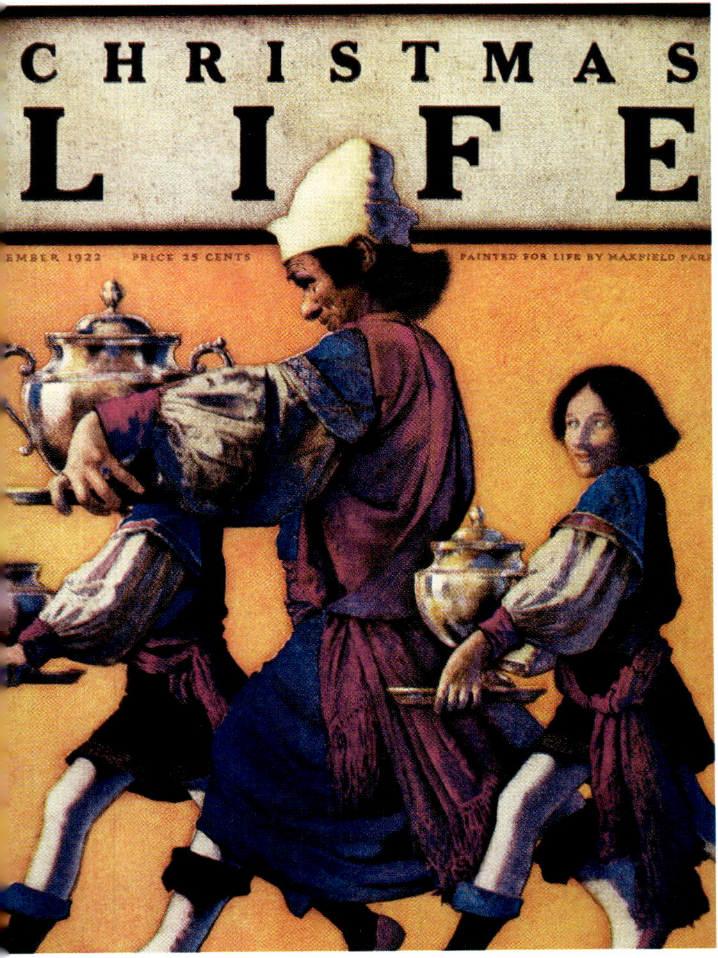
CHRISTMAS
LIFE
EMBER 1922
PRICE 25 CENTS
PAINTED FOR LIFE BY MAXFIELD PARR

Collier's
July 7, 1906

New Year, who is dressed in rain gear and holding a large umbrella. Other cover titles in this group include *The Gardener, The Pirate, The Botanist, The Book Lover,* and *Vaudeville*. Although Parrish ended his agreement with *Collier's* in 1910, Parrish covers appeared on the magazine for the next few years.

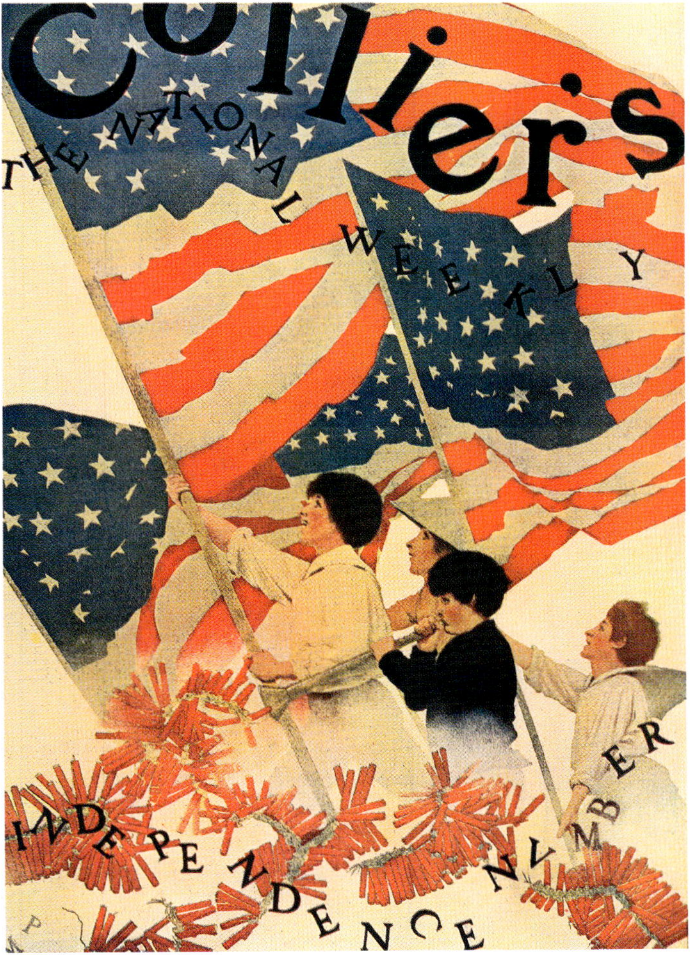
Collier's
THE NATIONAL WEEKLY
INDEPENDENCE NUMBER

Collier's
January 5, 1929

In 1911, Parrish was concentrating on a series of mural designs, when *Good Housekeeping Magazine* asked him to submit a set of illustrations. The series, based on fairy tales, ended up as covers of *Hearst Magazine,* a sister publication of *Good Housekeeping*. Although Parrish was not pleased with the magazine's mechanical manipulation of his art, the illustrations are splendid. *The Story of Snowdrop,*

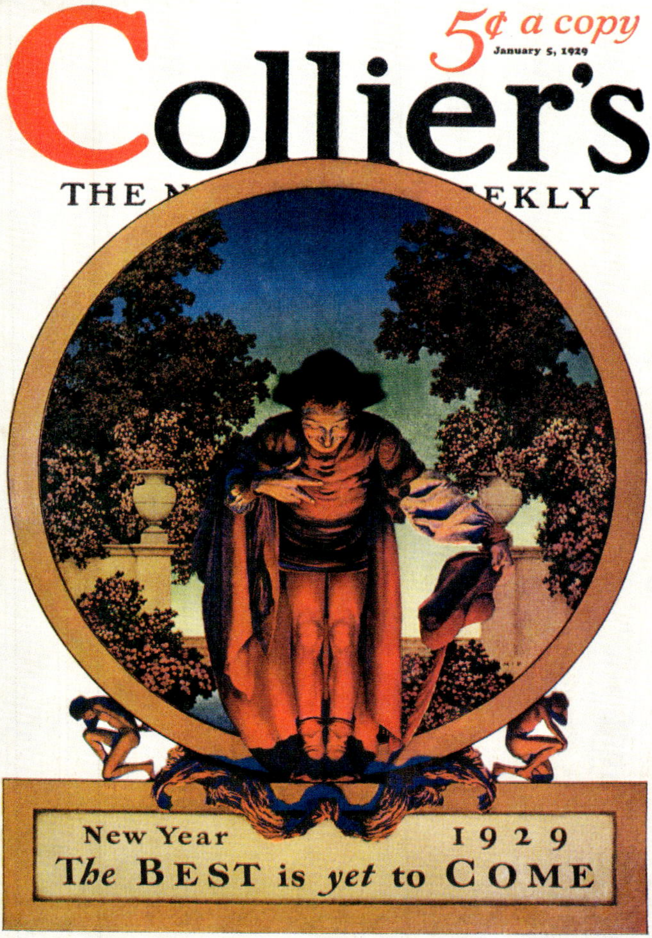
5¢ a copy
January 5, 1929
Collier's
THE
EKLY
New Year 1929
The BEST is yet to COME

Ladies' Home Journal

Christmas 1912

Sleeping Beauty, and the rest eloquently speak of Parrish's other-worldly fantasies.

Life, the humor magazine, was the last publication to which Parrish submitted a large body of work. (He designed covers for others after working for *Life,* but only sporadically.) Parrish completed a handful of covers for *Life* in the early 1900s. Starting in

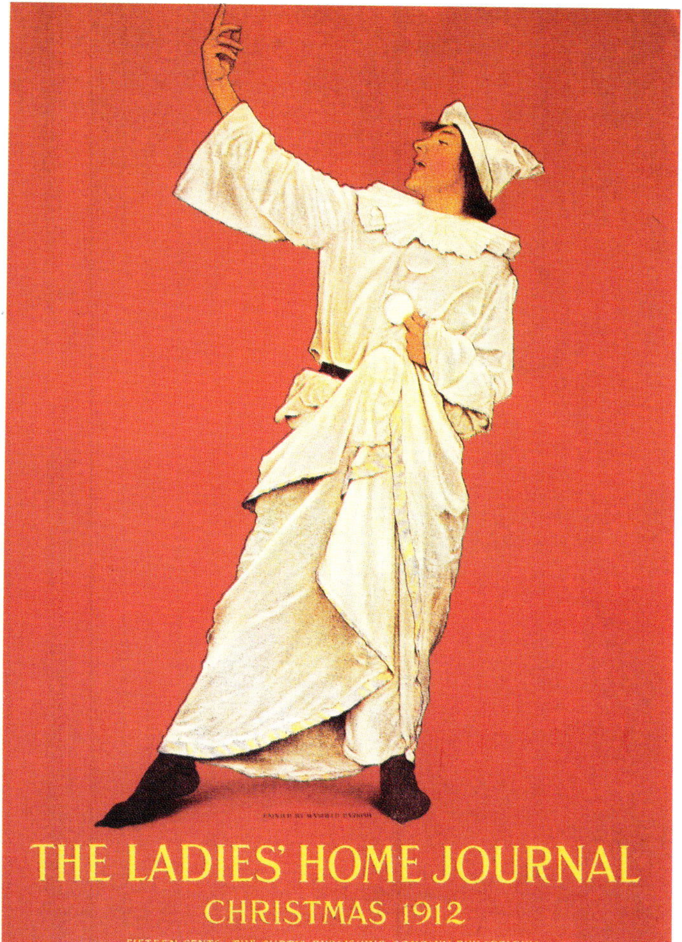
THE LADIES' HOME JOURNAL
CHRISTMAS 1912
FIFTEEN CENTS · THE CURTIS PUBLISHING COMPANY PHILADELPHIA

Metropolitan Magazine
January 1917

1920, Parrish covers appeared on more than a dozen *Life* magazines. For Parrish, this must have been similar to the soul-fulfilling work he did for *Collier's* – only better. Some covers feature images similar to his art prints like *Daybreak,* which were becoming extremely popular: *Morning* for the Easter 1922 issue and *The Canyon,* March 1923, are excellent examples of this style.

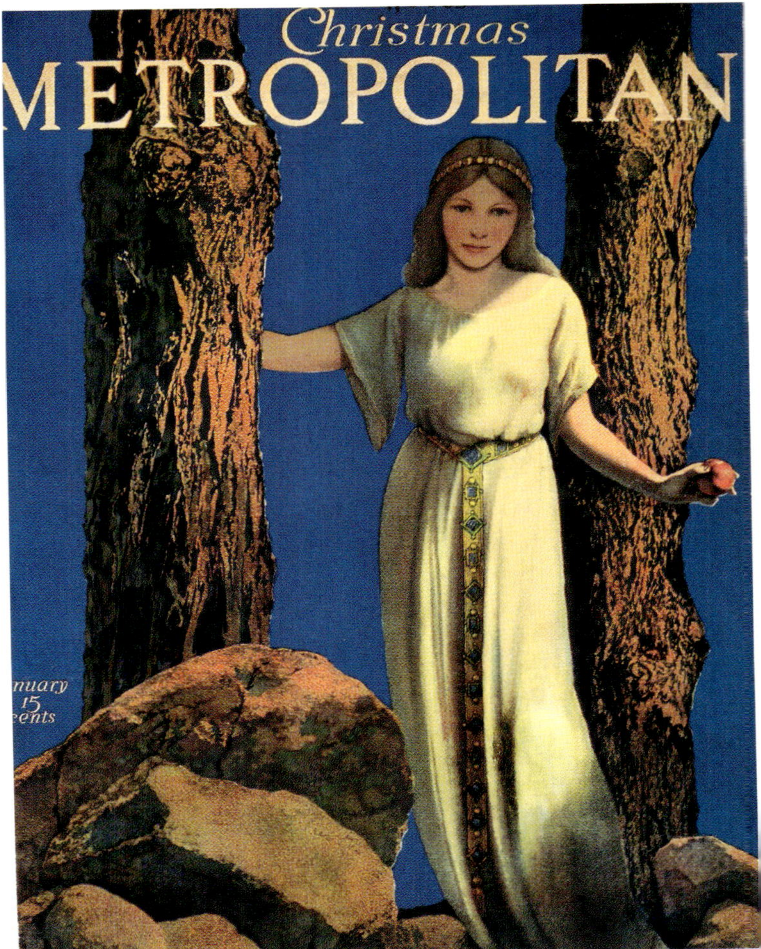
Christmas
METROPOLITAN
nuary
15
ents

Hearst's
May 1914

Parrish also continued use of comical figures, such as *The Swiss Admiral* and *A Dark Futurist*, set against white backgrounds on covers. For the *A Dark Futurist* cover, Parrish created a comical, gnome-like man with facial features decidedly similar to those of Parrish. This character also appears on a handful of other *Life* covers. Parrish employed allegorial subjects on other covers for the magazine: Saint Valentine,

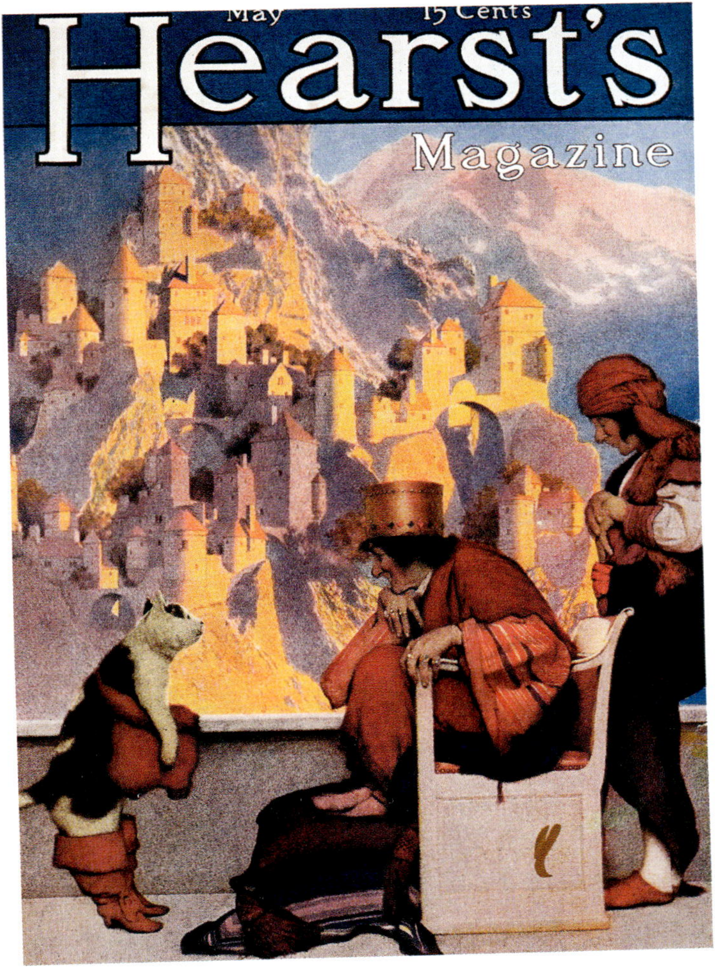
May
15 Cents
Hearst's
Magazine

The Ladies' Home Journal
July 1912

February 1905; Humpty Dumpty, a perennial favorite, for the Easter 1921 issue; and a fisherman, August 1921.

By the end of the 1920s, Parrish left the magazine field, with only occasional exceptions. He did covers in later years for *Collier's* and *Life,* as well as more eclectic publications such as *The New Hampshire Troubadour* (1935) and *The Progressive Farmer* (1952). But these represent a handful compared to his prolific earlier work.

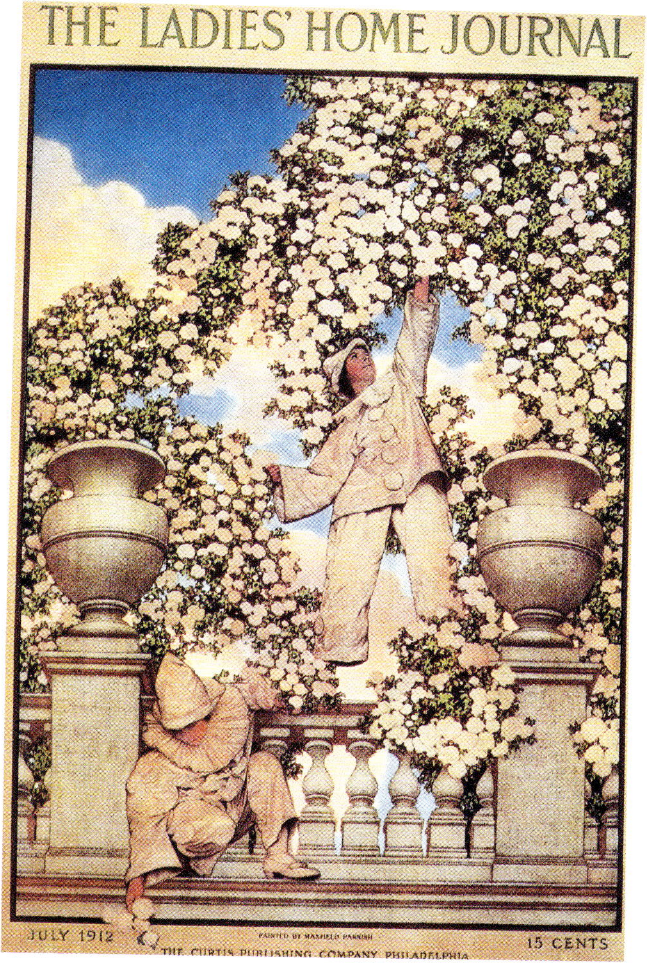
THE LADIES' HOME JOURNAL
JULY 1912
PAINTED BY MAXFIELD PARRISH
15 CENTS
THE CURTIS PUBLISHING COMPANY PHILADELPHIA

The Ladies' Home Journal

July 1896

Parrish's contribution to the art of magazine illustration cannot be overstated. It seemed each field of art he touched upon, he conquered. Many of his magazine covers were straightforward paintings appropriate for any cover. Many made their way into the art-print field and continue to be reprinted today as posters, calendars, and note cards.

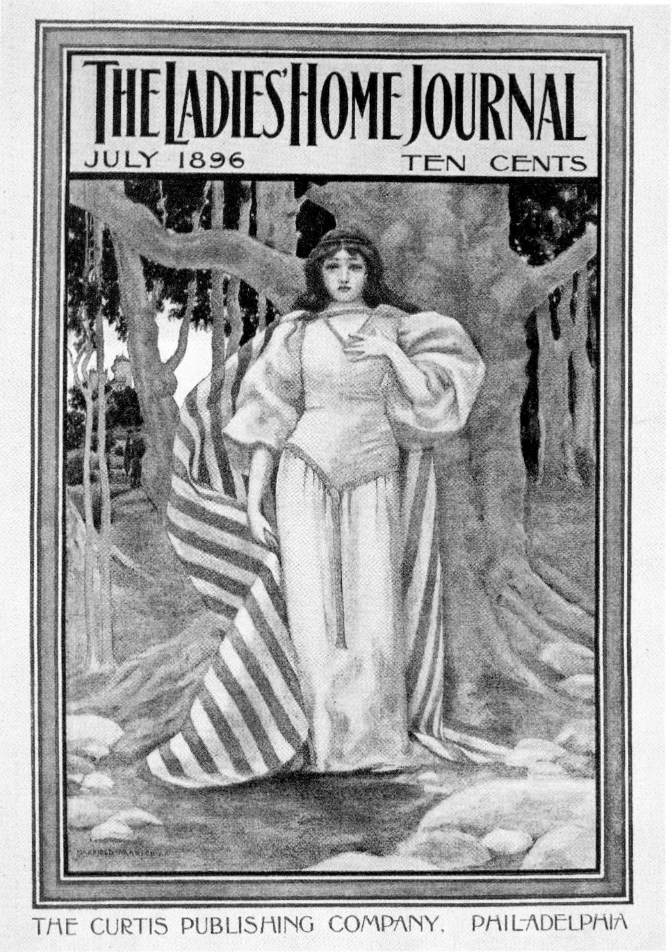
THE LADIES' HOME JOURNAL
JULY 1896
TEN CENTS
THE CURTIS PUBLISHING COMPANY. PHILADELPHIA

The Ladies' Home Journal
May 1913

Other covers, especially his later work, exhibit the artist's attempt to come to terms with the page's graphic structure. His comical covers are witty in the true sense of the word; there humor is never harsh but, instead, well thought out and universal. Today admirers and collectors are rediscovering many of Parrish's somewhat less

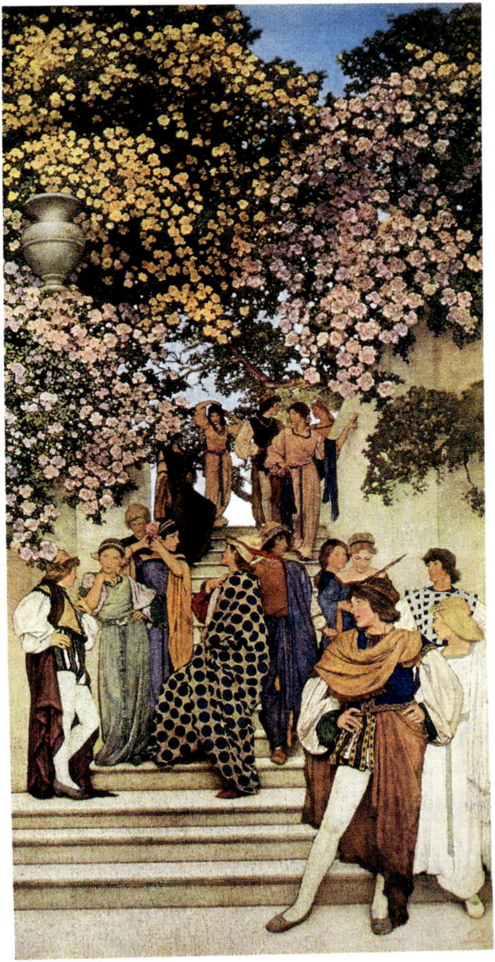

Life
August 25, 1921

popular covers. Although critics decried forays Parrish made into commercial art, his present-day faithful followers are less critical. For them, anything he created was beautiful.

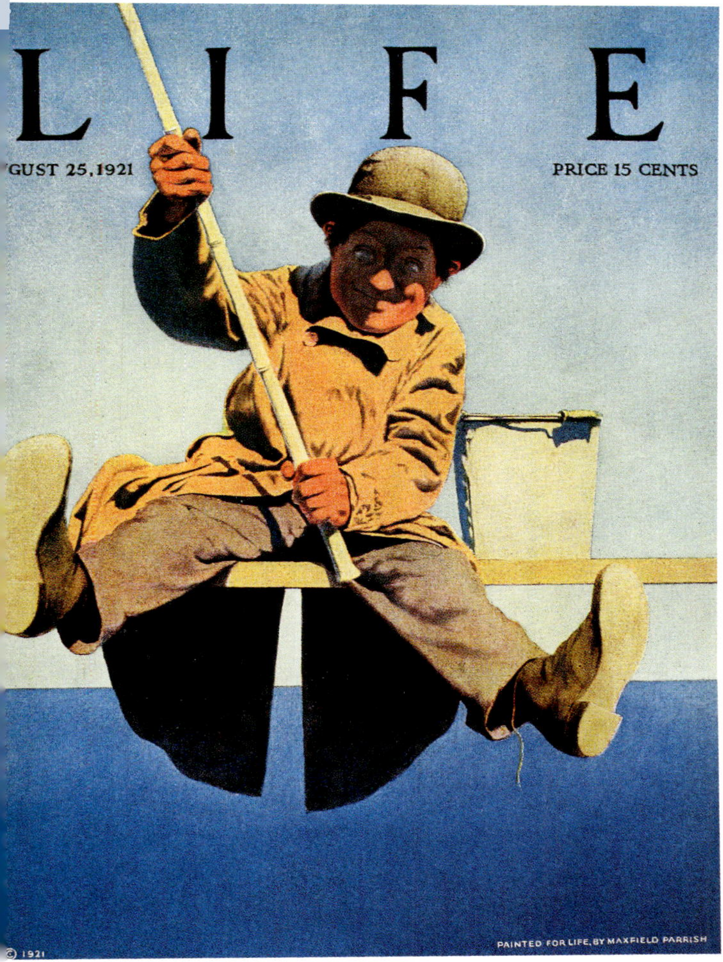
LIFE
GUST 25, 1921
PRICE 15 CENTS
© 1921
PAINTED FOR LIFE, BY MAXFIELD PARRISH

Vignettes

Vignettes

Vignettes

MAXFIELD PARRISH

THE BOOK ILLUSTRATIONS

Michael J. Goldberg

Collectors Press, Inc.
Portland, Oregon

Acknowledgements

Collection courtesy of Erwin Flacks, Fine Art Marketing Co., and the archives of Collectors Press, Inc.

Editor:
Michael J. Goldberg

Design:
Hoover H.Y. Li

Copyright © 1998 Collectors Press, Inc.

All rights reserved. No part of this book may be reproduced or transmitted in any form or by any means, electronic or mechanical, including photocopying, recording, or by any information storage and retrieval system, without written permission from Collectors Press, Inc.

Published by: Collectors Press, Inc.
P.O. Box 230986, Portland, OR 97281
1-800-423-1848

Printed in Singapore

First American Edition

10 9 8 7 6 5 4 3 2 1

ISBN: 1-888054-21-2

Maxfield Parrish

"And what is the use of a book" thought Alice, "without pictures."

Alice's Adventures in Wonderland, Lewis Carroll

Indeed, as Alice remarked, viewing her older sister's book before embarking on her adventures in Wonderland, books need pictures – especially those directed toward children. When Alice made her classic observation, not many adults were making books for children. Early Victorian children likely read books heavy with morals and sponsored by the Church of England. Critics have called *Alice's Adventures in Wonderland* a parody and political critique. In reality, it was written as a child's story. It was the first children's fantasy book to become widely popular.

Carroll's *Alice* appeared at the dawn of a technological revolution. With advances in printing processes allowing color reproduction, book publishing became a thriving industry. Nowhere did creative expression flourish as fully as in fantasy illustration. In areas such as poetry, classics,

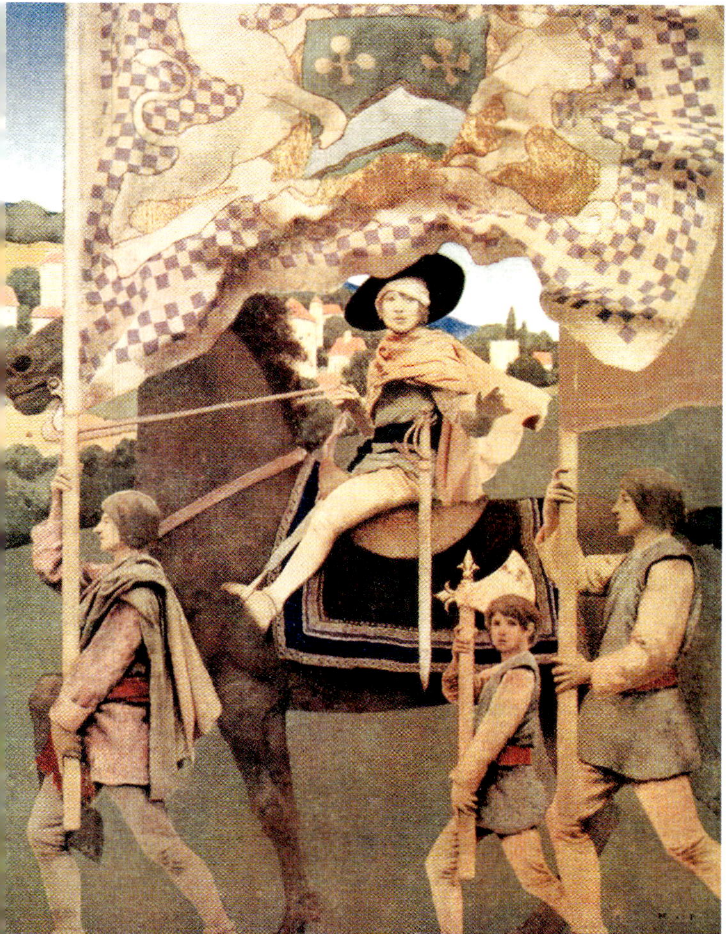

and children's books, creative artists found blank canvases on which to express their inner visions. The huge buying public eagerly purchased this commodity – available to many for the first time.

The demand for illustrators literally created a new field of employment. Many of the Victorian era children's illustrators rose to prominence – Sir John Tenniel, whose illustrations for

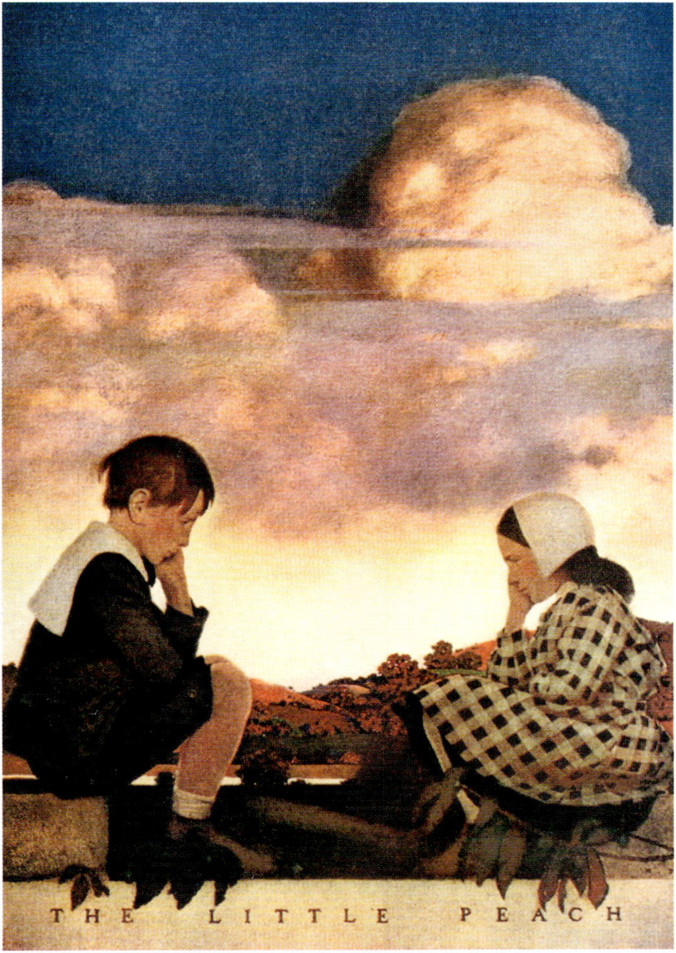
THE LITTLE PEACH

The Fisherman and the Genie
The Arabian Nights
1909

the original *Alice's Adventures in Wonderland,* have become classics; Randolph Caldecott, for whom the Caldecott Award for children's illustration is named; Kate Greenaway, who created her own world with her familiar children's drawings; Walter Crane, whose "Toy Books" series first appeared in 1865 – these were some of the earliest. By the turn of the century,

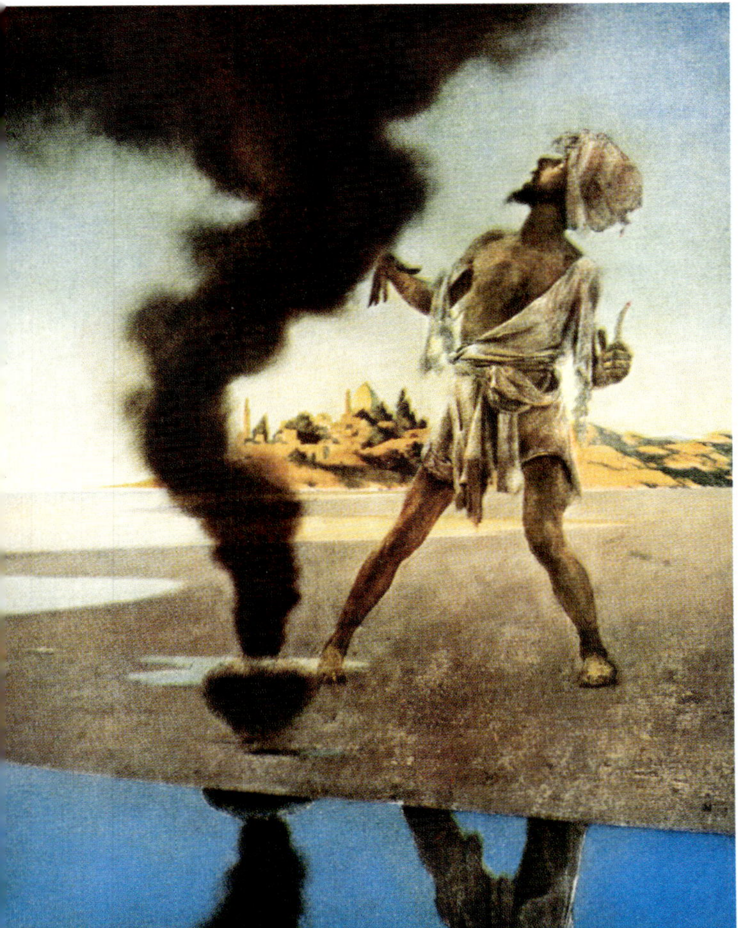

The Reluctant Dragon
Dream Days
1898

England was producing fantasy illustrators like Arthur Rackham, Edmund Dulac, and Aubrey Beardsley.

During this time, America still looked toward England for styles and trends. The incredible amount of illustrated art coming out of Great Britain could not be denied. Into this period Maxfield Parrish was born. Surely many books that Parrish read as a child were published in England.

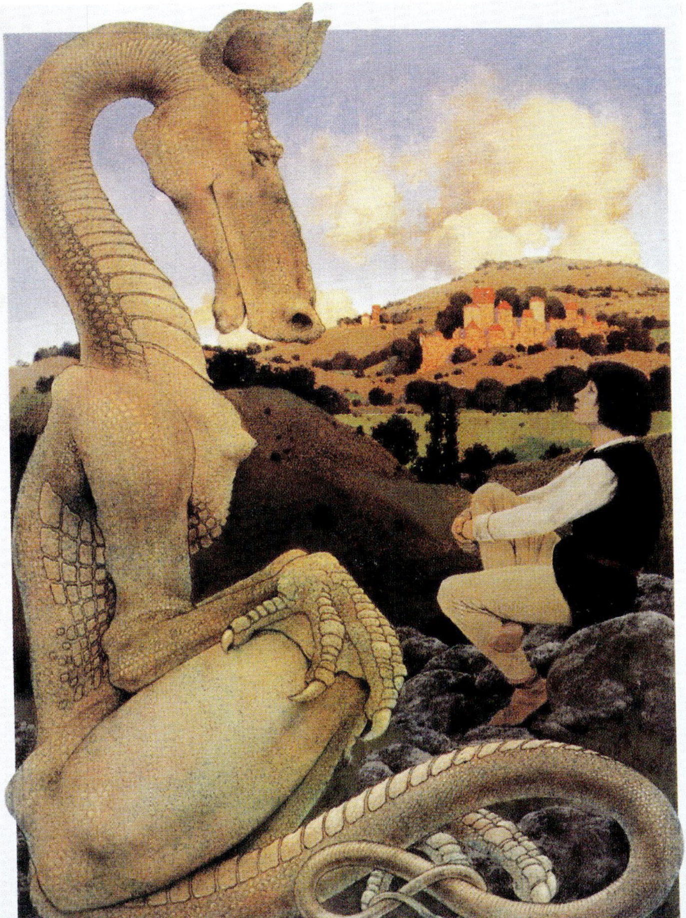

Cassim
The Arabian Nights
1909

Children's books printed in America were still somewhat crude, though readily available and inexpensive. By the time Parrish was making great strides in his career as an illustrator, he would also be making great contributions to children's book illustration in its Golden Age.

Parrish contributed his early black-and-white artwork to such books as *Mother Goose in Prose, Dream Days,*

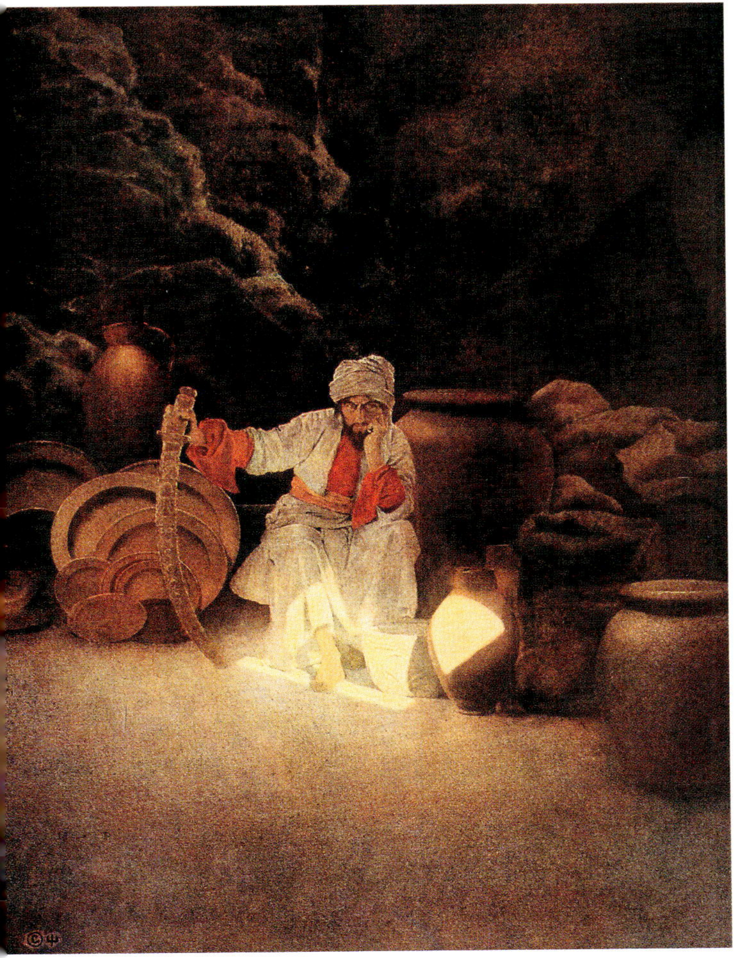

Atlas
A Wonder Book and Tanglewood Tales
1910

and *The Golden Age*. The character of Mother Goose and the vision of the world as seen by a child was perfectly captured by Parrish's illustrations. When Parrish moved into his color-illustration period, his style blossomed. His book career culminated in *The Knave of Hearts*. These illustrations captured the essence of the Parrish style.

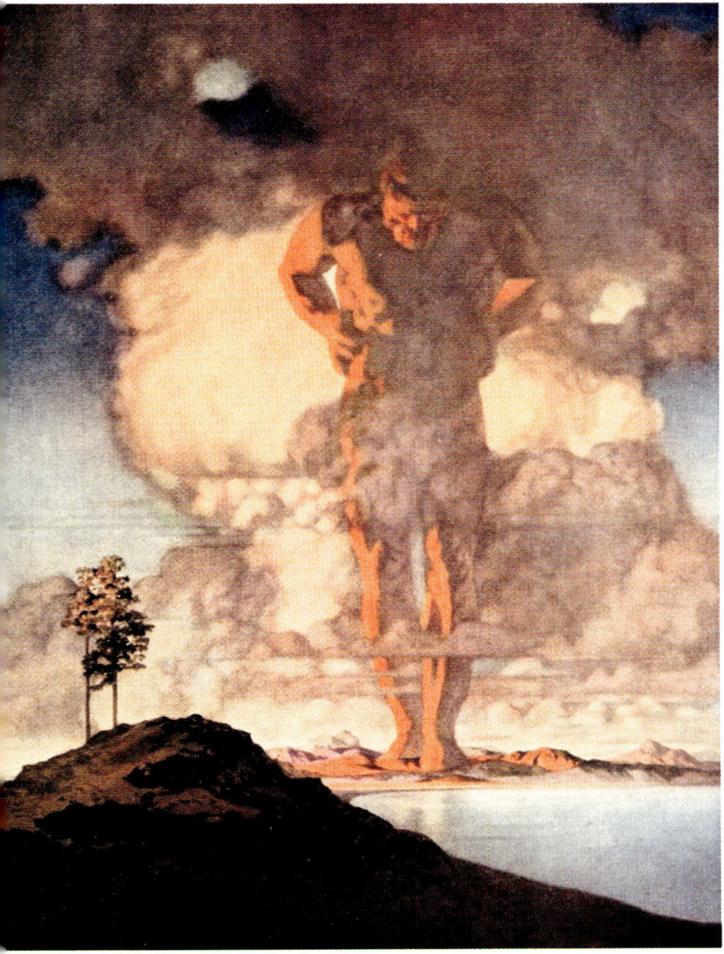

Jason and the Talking Oak
A Wonder Book and Tanglewood Tales
1910

Parrish's career in book illustration began on a positive note. His first illustrated book was *Mother Goose in Prose* published in 1897 by Way and Williams. The author was none other than L. Frank Baum, who achieved fame a few years later as the creator of the Wizard of Oz. *Mother Goose in Prose* was a collection of whimsical prose stories based on nursery rhymes. Parrish contributed a full-color cover

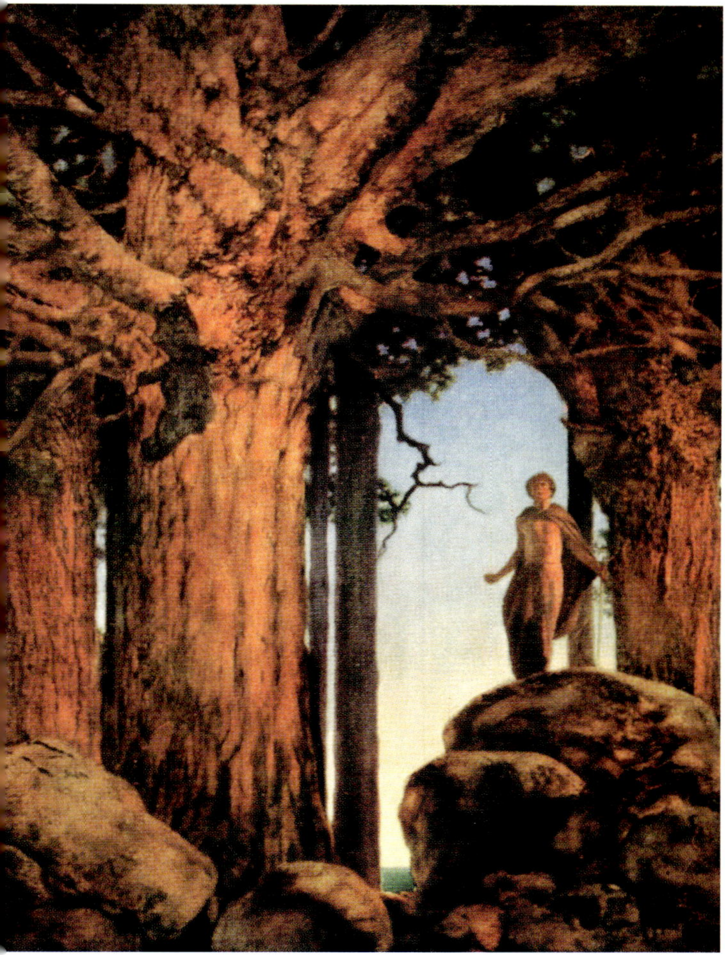

Its Walls Were as of Jasper
Dream Days
1898

and fourteen black-and-white illustrations. The combination of author and illustrator produced a book that became a huge success, with several printings in later years. The black-and-white illustrations make strong use of texture and design to produce wonderful images. Many Mother Goose characters dear to Parrish are featured here: Old King Cole, Little

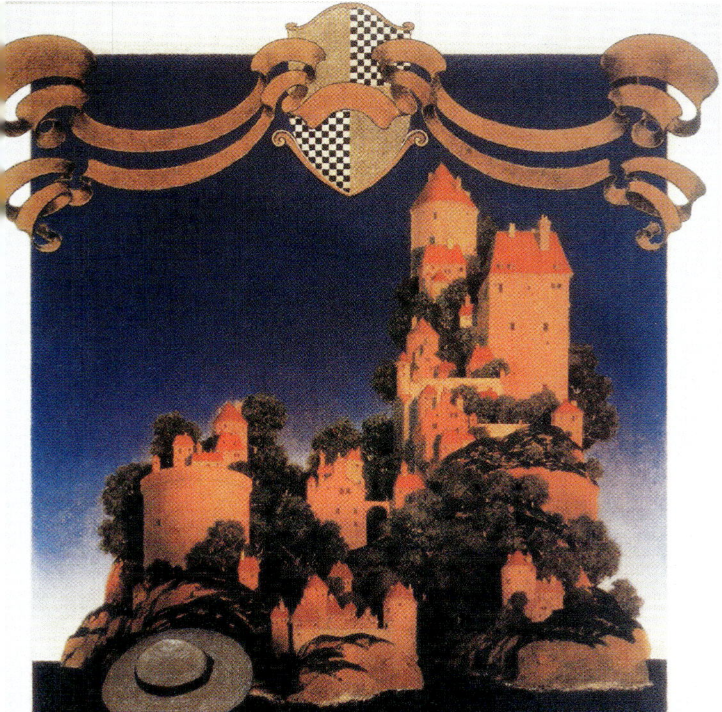

Bo-Peep, The Man in the Moon, and Humpty Dumpty, whose broad smile has become a familiar image.

After the success of *Mother Goose in Prose,* Parrish's major book commissions came annually for the next few years. He literally started the next assignment as he neared the end of the previous book. He dovetailed the book commissions into his schedule of advertising and magazine assignments.

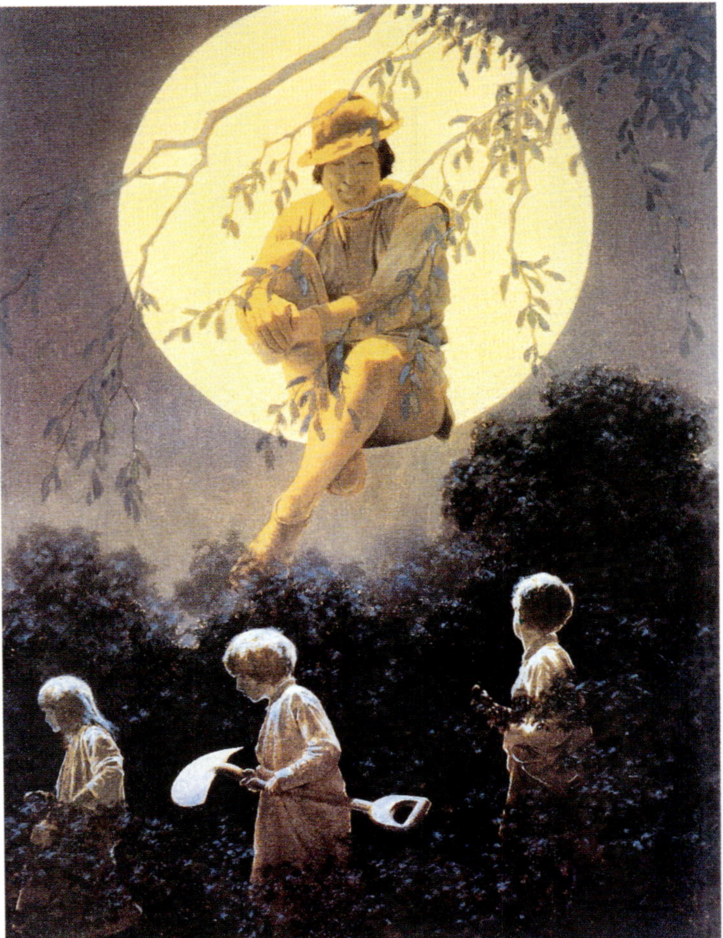

With Trumpet and Drum
Poems of Childhood
1904

Parrish was proficient in creating on a tight schedule, and, in 1900, *Knickerbocker's History of New York* by Washington Irving was released with Parrish illustrations. A whimsical parody of old New York written one hundred years earlier, Parrish's illustrations were perfectly suited for the book because of his personal depiction of the characters.

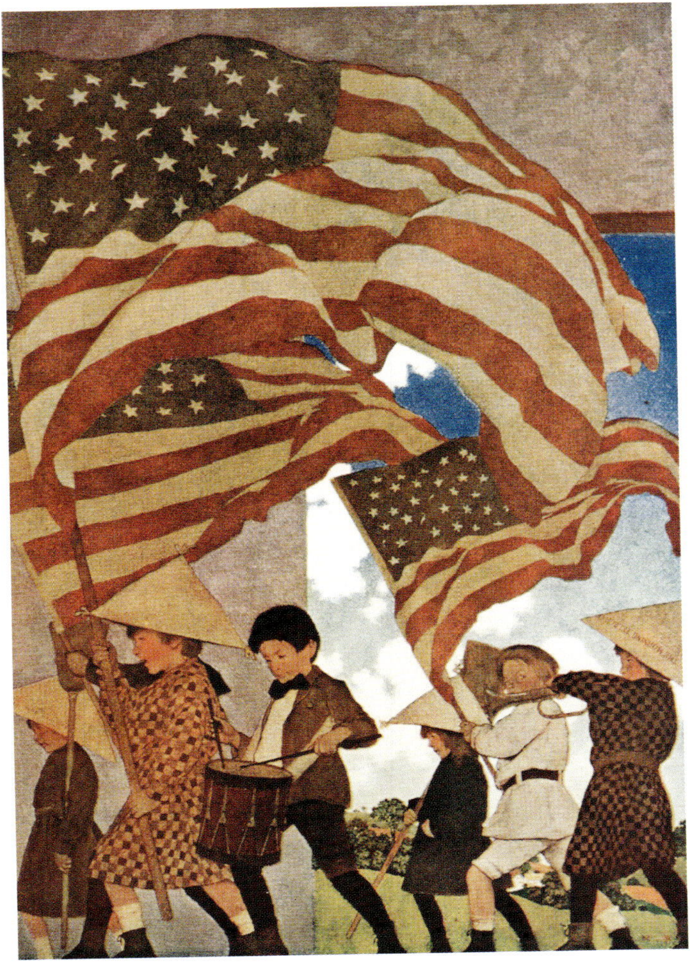

Search for the Singing Tree
The Arabian Nights
1909

Parrish's next two book commissions were *The Golden Age* and its sequel *Dream Days,* both by Kenneth Grahame. These two books featured the world viewed through a child's mind and imagination. Both explore childlike fantasies of dragons and castles, mysterious gardens, wandering roads, and adults who appear as gods of mythology. Parrish's pictures of

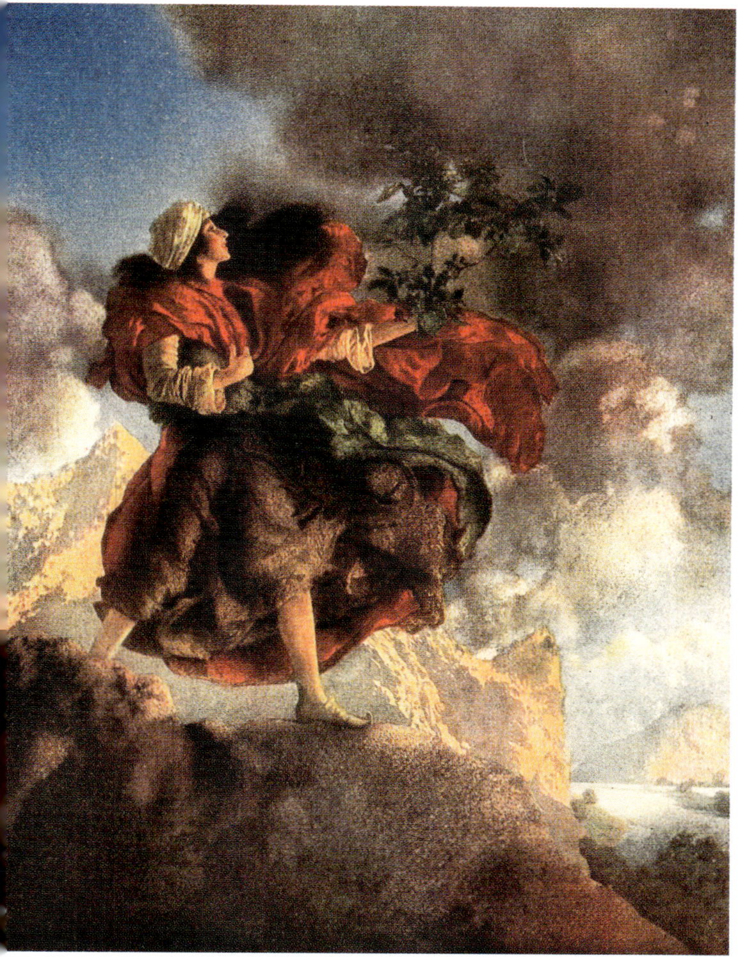

The Cardinal Archbishop
The Turquoise Cup and the Desert
1903

children set among their imaginings are neither coy nor idealized. Like Dorothy, who casually strolled through Oz, the children of Parrish's work seem believable as they move through their fantasies. *The Golden Age* was the first of Parrish's books to become popular in Europe. The British in particular, who had spearheaded the book illustration movement, were taken by the Parrish style when *The*

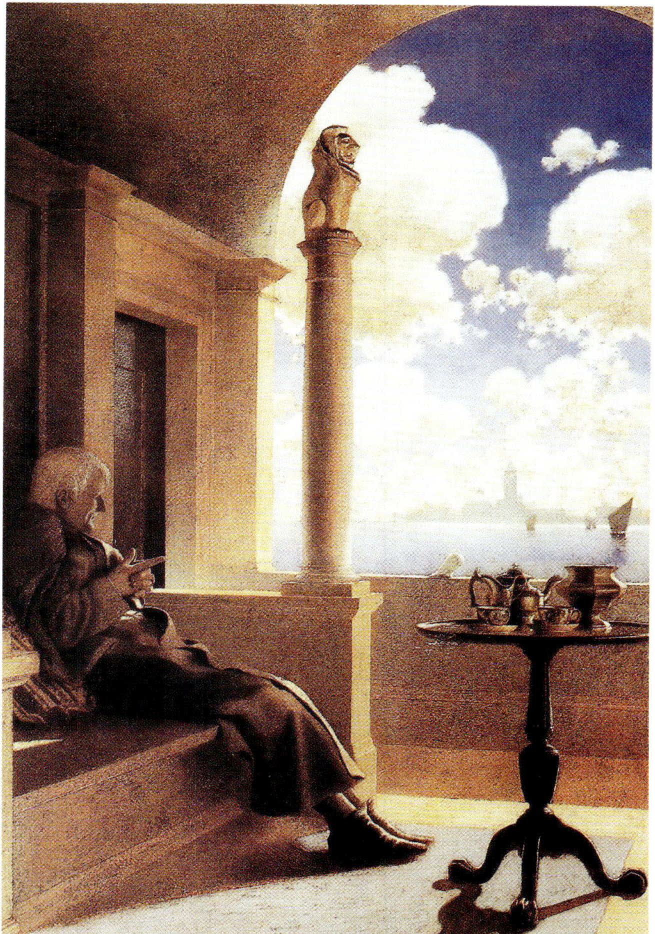

The Reservoir
Italian Villas and Their Gardens
1904

Golden Age was published in London simultaneously with its release in America. This overseas recognition expanded Parrish's devoted audience beyond its American boundaries.

The next book Parrish illustrated was a milestone in his book illustration career. *Poems of Childhood,* by noted American poet Eugene Field, was Parrish's first full-color book and became the children's book for which

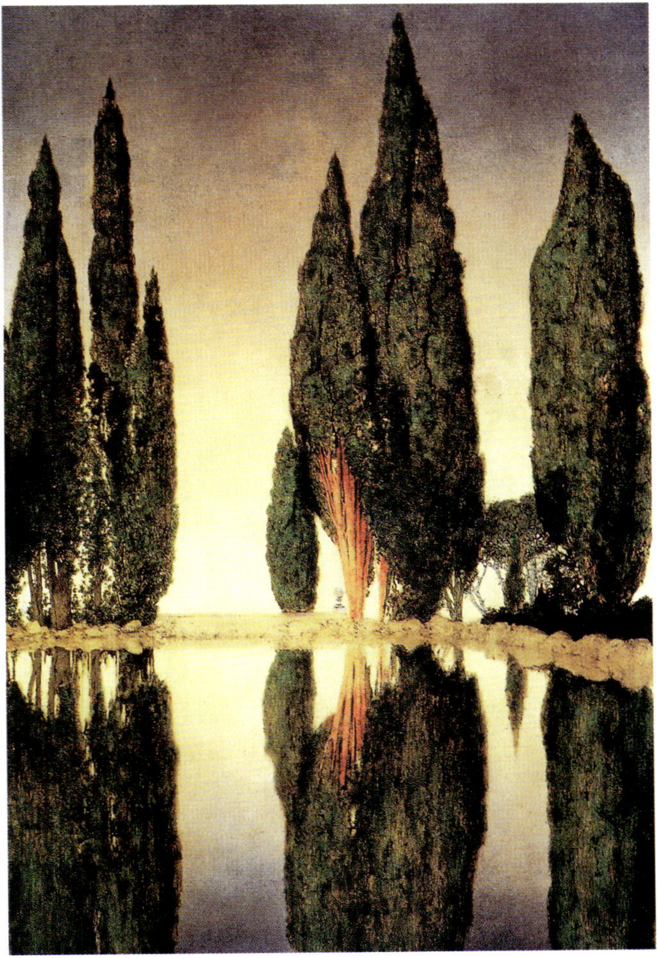

Villa Scassi

Italian Villas and Their Gardens

1904

he is most remembered. Originally appearing in the *Ladies' Home Journal,* the idea was quickly expanded by the publisher into book form published in fall 1904. Parrish provided eight full-page illustrations, as well as the cover and miscellaneous pieces of art. Field's poems, particularly "Wynken, Blynken and Nod" and "The Sugar-Plum Tree," were already children's favorites and Parrish's illustrations still appear in

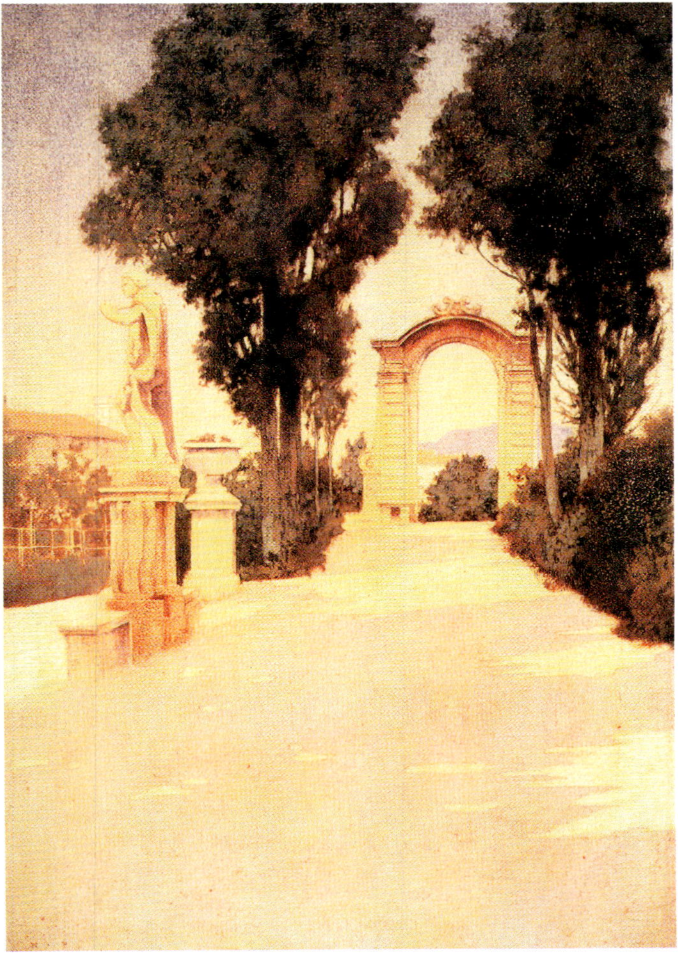

Ye Royall Recepcioun
Whist Reference Book
1897

poetry anthologies. Parrish again used his personal vision, inspired by the poems, to illustrate the works, delivering stunning pieces rife with his dreamlike quality. Most notable is the illustration called *The Dinkey-Bird*. In it, a maiden on a swing sails past billowing clouds and a castle-crowned mountain top. *The Dinkey-Bird* pulls

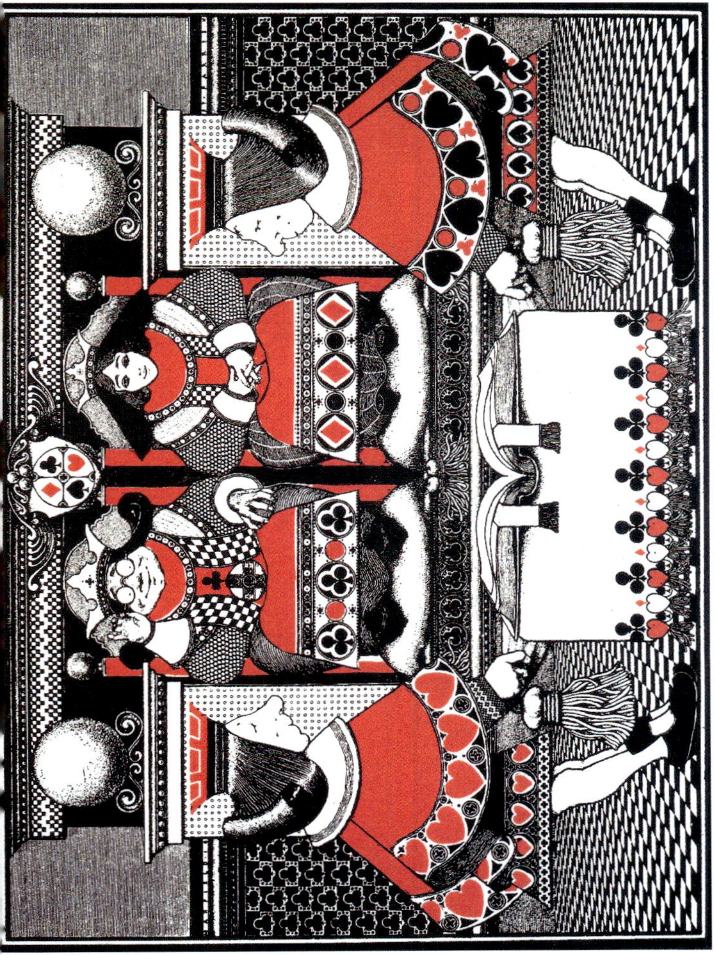

The Argonauts in Quest of the Golden Fleece
A Wonder Book and Tanglewood Tales
1910

together a Parrish theme that re-appeared time and time again, without swing.

Further Parrish book commissions continued, grown from illustration jobs originally created for magazines. Parrish's next book project began as one such magazine assignment. This book was to be a departure in subject matter from his usual images of fancy. First serialized in the *Century Magazine,*

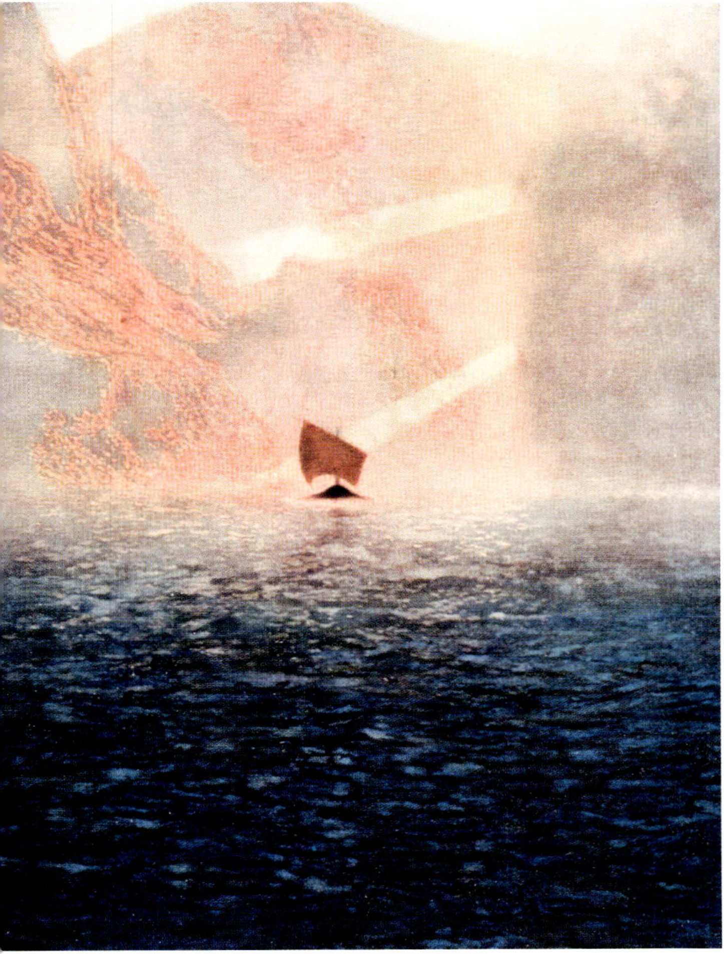

Bellerophon by the Fountain of Pirene
A Wonder Book and Tanglewood Tales
1910

Italian Villas and Their Gardens appeared in 1904 in book form. Written by noted American novelist Edith Wharton, the volume was a collaboration based on the author's and illustrator's research in Italy (although they did not travel together). The result was an interesting book that pleased the author and gave Parrish a chance to break from his usual works and

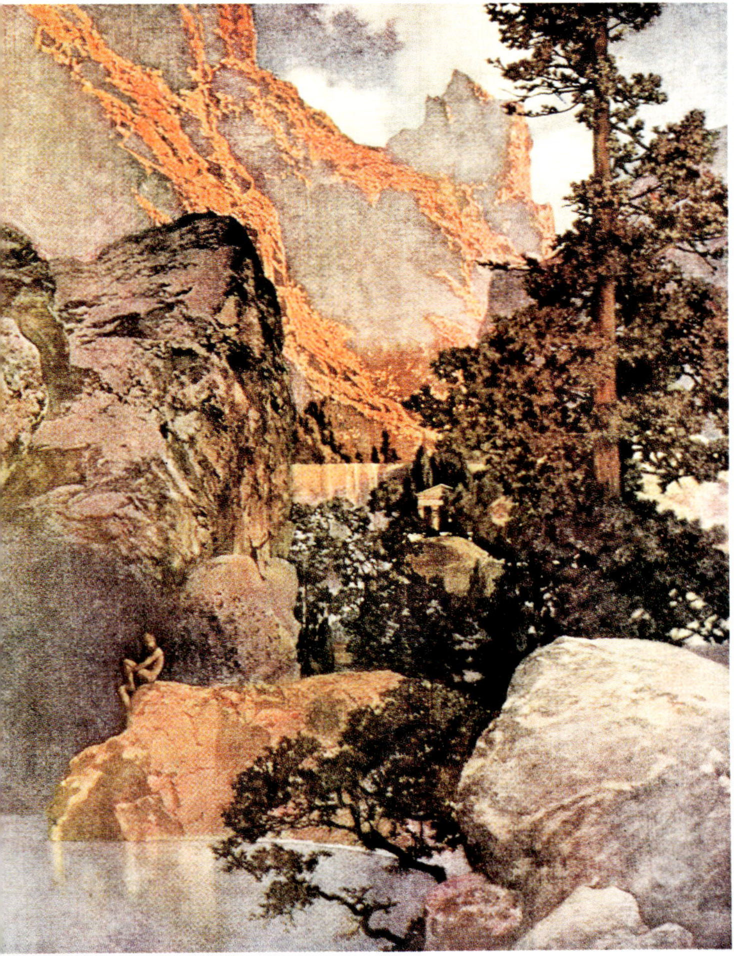

The Pastry Cooks
The Knave of Hearts
1925

concentrate on detailed architectural renderings. The numerous illustrations for this book are more than renderings of buildings. Parrish incorporates landscape elements with his Parrish-blue skies to produce some beautifully evocative paintings. Not as widely known as his children's books, *Italian Villas* is no less intriguing in the Parrish pantheon.

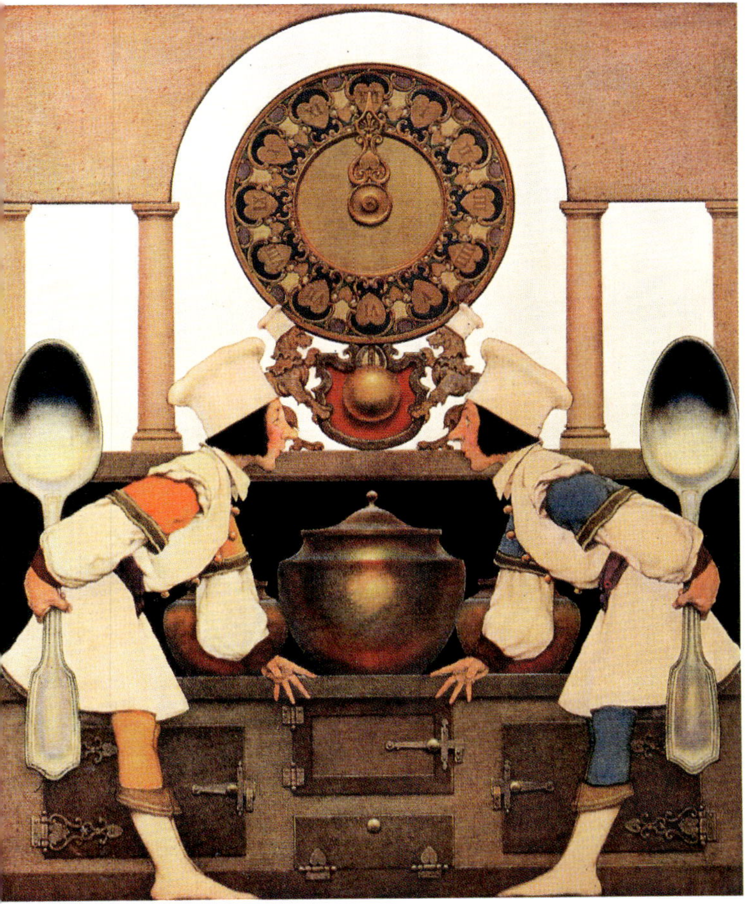

King Pompdebile
The Knave of Hearts
1925

Parrish's next two books wandered into the realm of the mythological and both originated as magazine illustrations. *The Arabian Nights* first appeared in *Collier's* magazine and in book form in 1909. Besides depicting popular tales such as "Aladdin," "Ali Baba," and "Sinbad," Parrish illuminated lesser known tales with beautiful illustrations. *Prince Agib, Search for the*

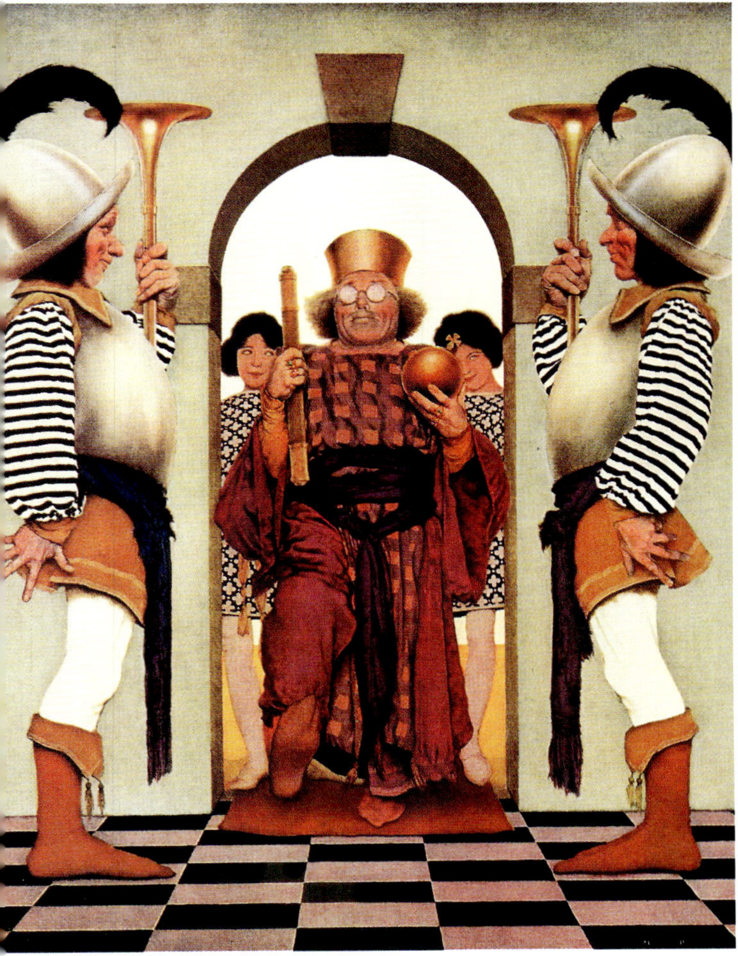

King and Violetta
The Knave of Hearts
1925

Singing Tree, and *The King of the Black Isles* have become recognizable classics from this book.

The following year, the release of *A Wonder Book and Tanglewood Tales* brought to book form the illustrations Parrish had done for *Collier's* under the name *Greek Mythology*. Nathaniel Hawthorne's books, first published in the 1850s, were a series of Greek

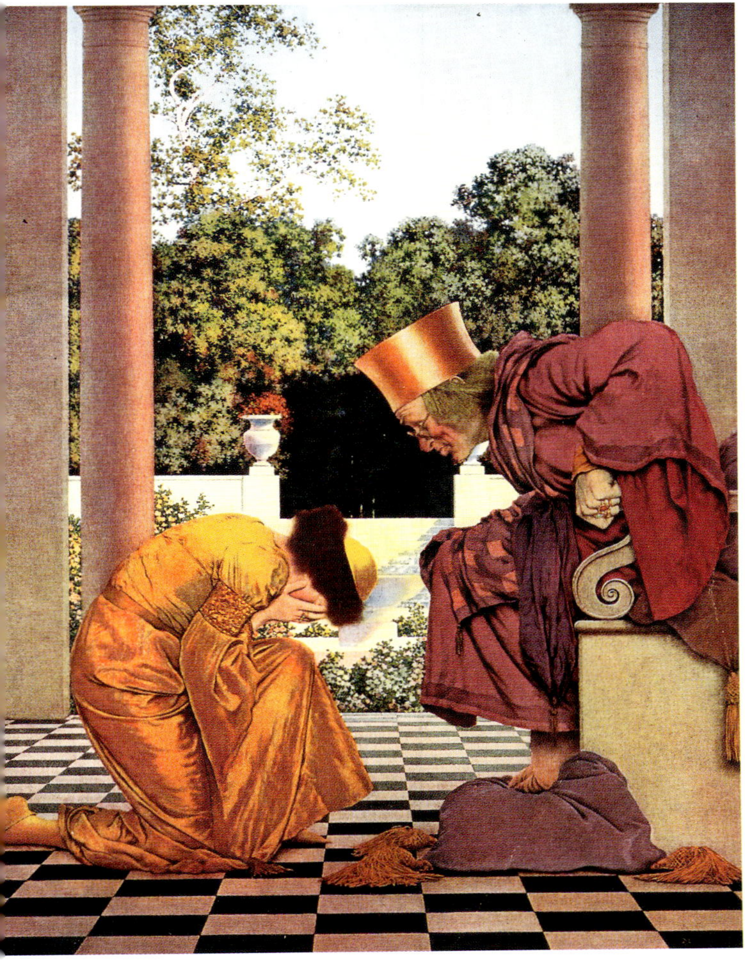

Six Young Servants
The Knave of Hearts
1925

myths retold for children. Parrish's paintings for the book are not only remarkable illustrations, but intense visual studies of shadow and light. Some illustrations like *The Fountain of Pirene* and *Circe's Palace* are mostly engulfed in shadows with one fixed distant light source. *Cadmus* and *Jason and His Teacher,* on the other hand, glow with brilliance as if lit by the

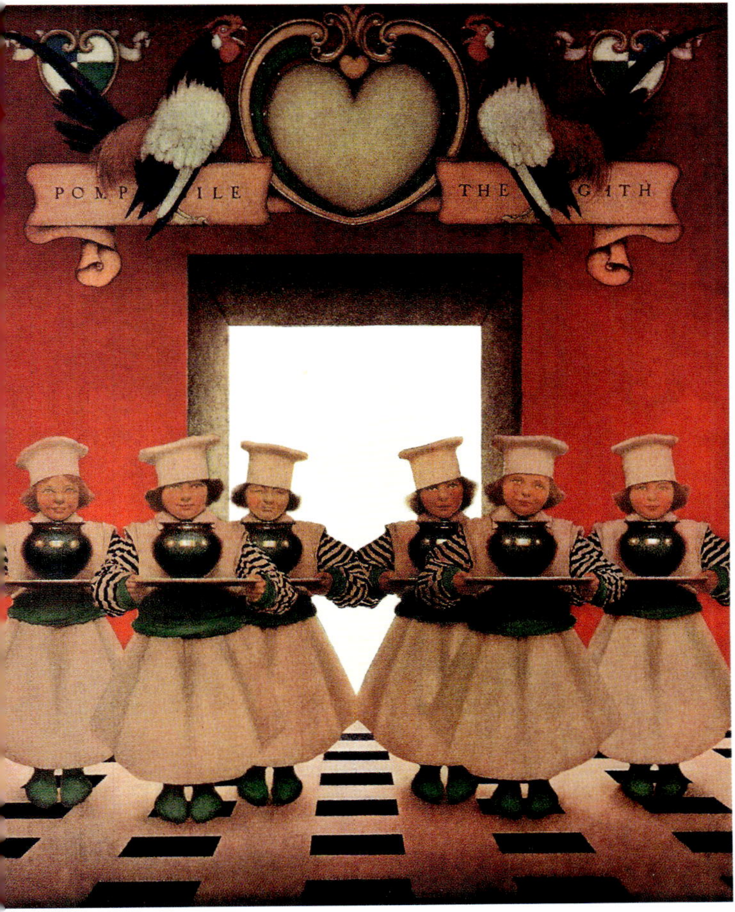
POMP ILE
THE

The Knave and Violetta
The Knave of Hearts
1925

bright rays of an orange setting sun. In fact, warm hues like oranges and yellows are placed beside dark shadowy tones in many of the illustrations for this book as well as for *The Arabian Nights*.

Parrish's greatest (and final) book project came fifteen years later. Parrish had done some paintings called "Once Upon a Time." They sat unused until Parrish discovered a play

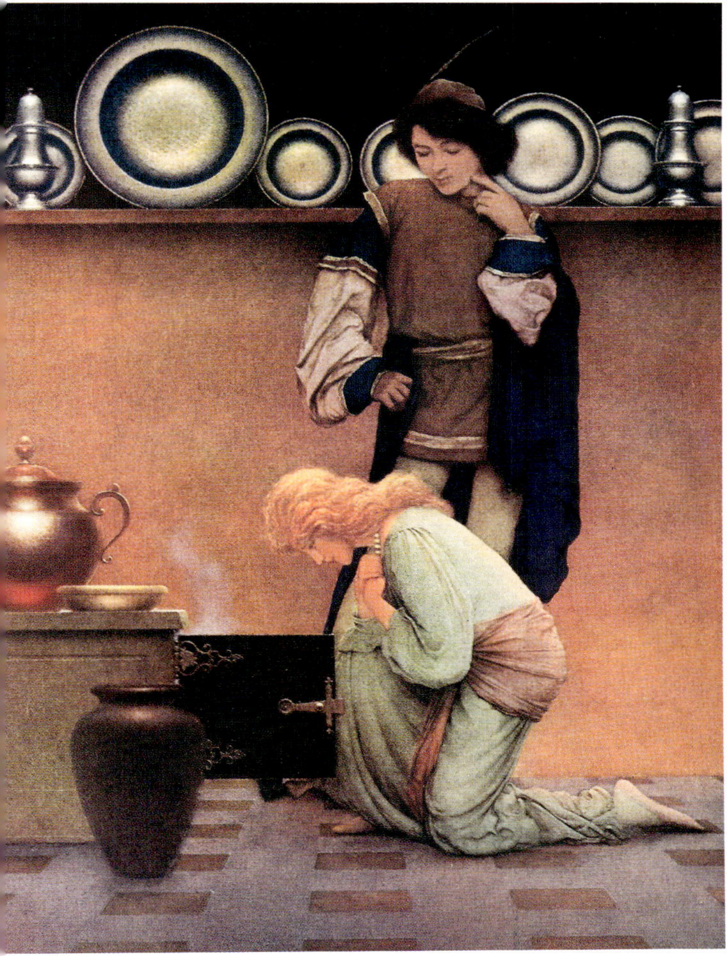

The Chancellor and King Pompdebile
The Knave of Hearts
1925

for children called "The Knave of Hearts." This was based, of course, on the nursery rhyme. Parrish was inspired by the dramatic content of the story and convinced his publisher to proceed with the project. *The Knave of Hearts* was released in 1925, resplendent with twenty-six beautiful color paintings. Besides the art, this was an over-the-top production featuring a

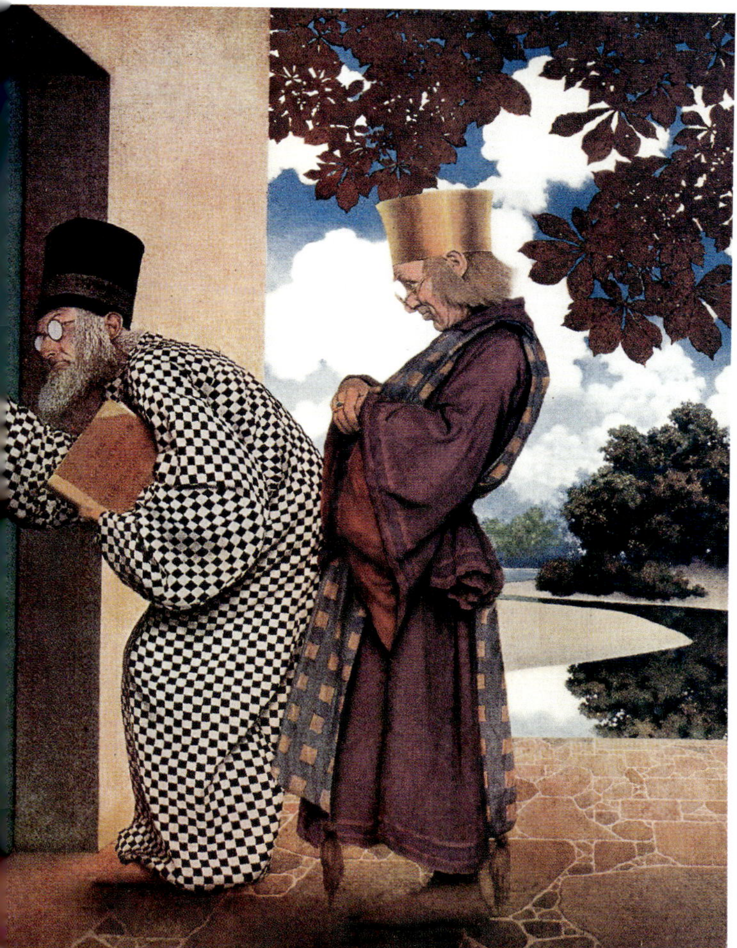

The Musician
The Knave of Hearts
1925

large-format book, its own box, and high-quality reproductions on high-grade paper. The publisher spared no expense, and extensive publicity aroused such interest that an exhibit of original Parrish art was mounted in New York, featuring the originals from *The Knave of Hearts*.

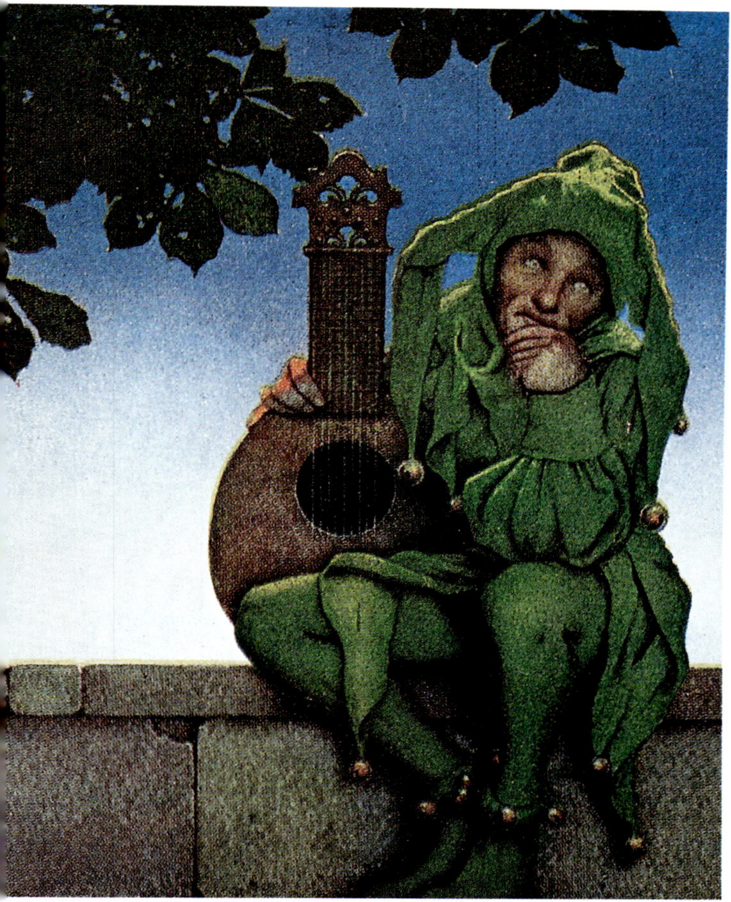

King, Chancellor and Pastry Cook

The Knave of Hearts

1925

No one can contest that these illustrations represent some of Parrish's best work – or at least that which we most frequently associate with Parrish. The highly stylized poses of the figures, both symmetric and not, and the fairy-tale landscape evoke the play and its subject perfectly. The theatrical element is also present in the

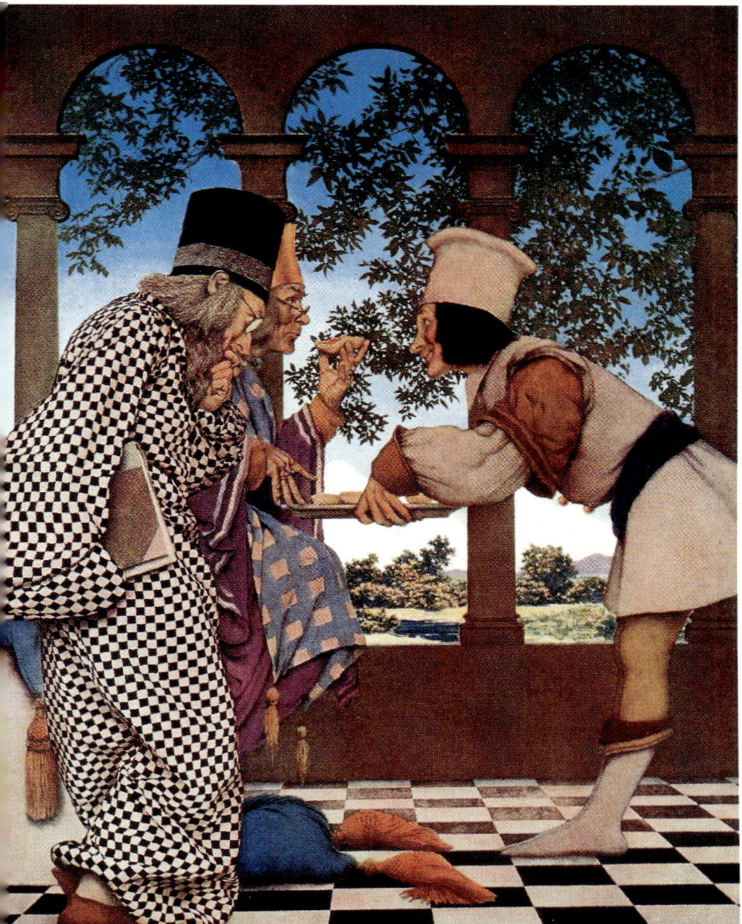

The End
The Knave of Hearts
1925

opening and closing illustrations of *The Manager,* seen drawing the curtain in the beginning and taking a bow on the end page. Another illustration in this book contains the famous *Chef Between Two Lobsters* and *The Pastry Cooks* with oversized spoons. Perhaps even more important is the cover lining painting called *Romance,* depicting a breathtaking landscape of

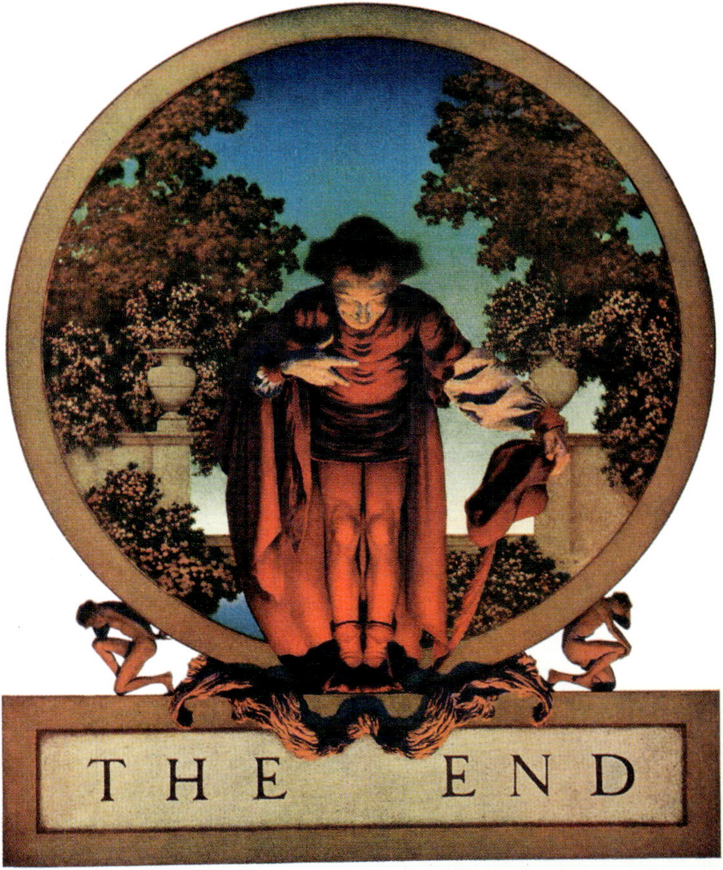
THE END

Autumn
The Golden Treasury of Songs and Lyrics
1911

river, mountains, and castles. *Romance* became one of the many book and magazine illustrations by Parrish to enter the art print market in the 1920s.

Though the public acclaim for the artwork was overwhelming, sales of the book were mediocre. The high quality of the book dictated a ten dollar price tag – quite a lot for a children's book back then. Books

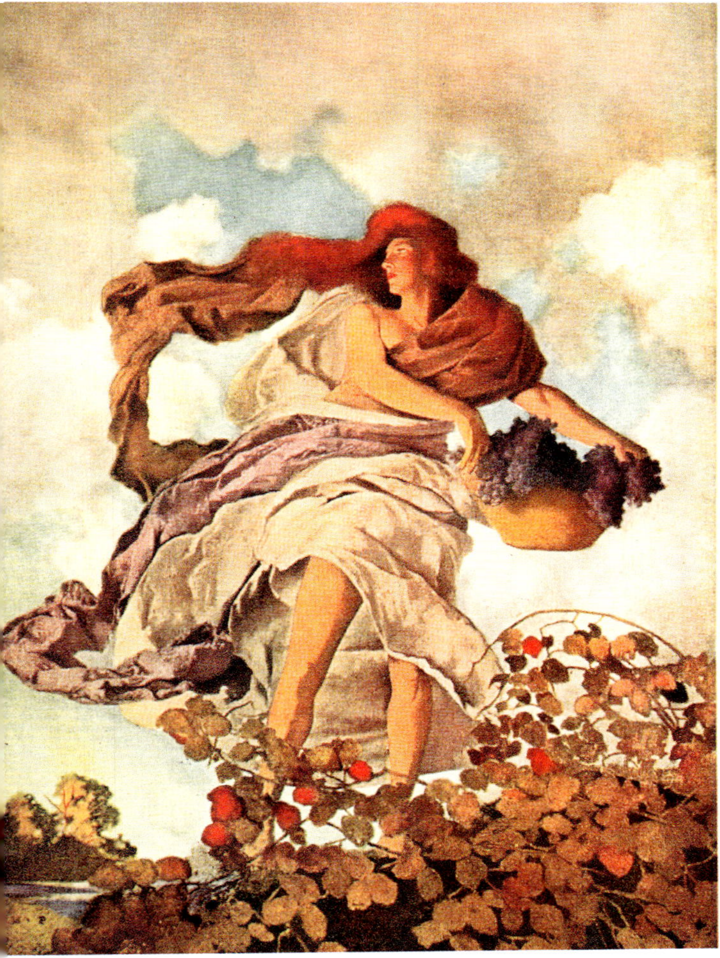

The Three Shepherds
The Golden Treasury of Songs and Lyrics
1911

printed in nonstandard book size are said to not sell as well and this was also the cause of the *Knave's* poor sales. Quite possibly, too, the beautiful illustrations were too complex and dramatic to appeal to a child. The low sales must have affected Parrish, who was used to more universal acceptance of his work.

By this time, Parrish was acquiring his fame and fortune from his art

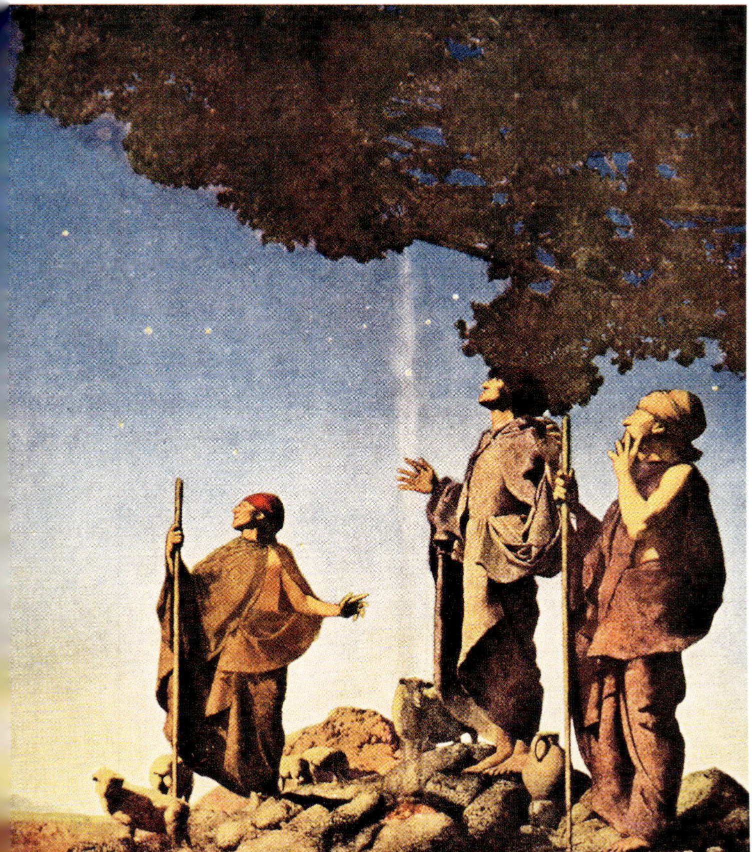

Spring
The Golden Treasury of Songs and Lyrics
1911

prints. Some were created for this market, while others were reprints from book and magazine illustrations.

Parrish eventually tired of the art print market as well, even though he controlled the subject matter. In 1930, Parrish left the world of commercial art – posters, ads, magazine, and book illustration – and went into semi-retirement. He entered one last agree-

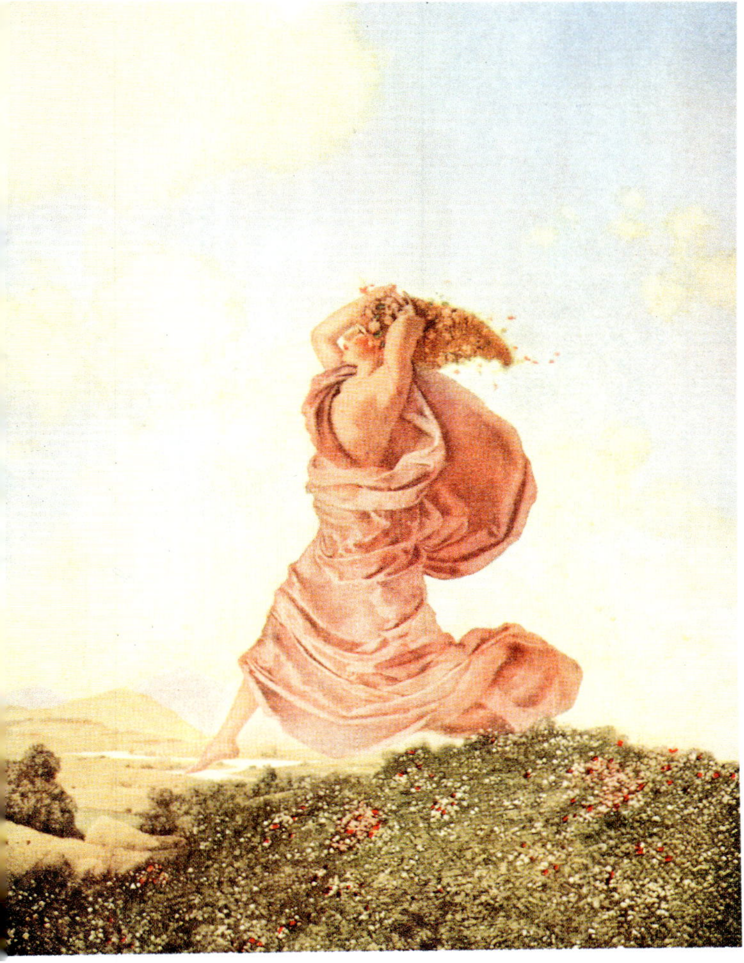

Easter
The Golden Treasury of Songs and Lyrics
1911

ment and submitted one painting a year to Brown & Bigelow, the famous calendar printing company. These paintings consisted of bucolic New England landscapes, without any hint of the fantastic and colorful book illustrations Maxfield Parrish contributed to the Golden Age of Illustration.

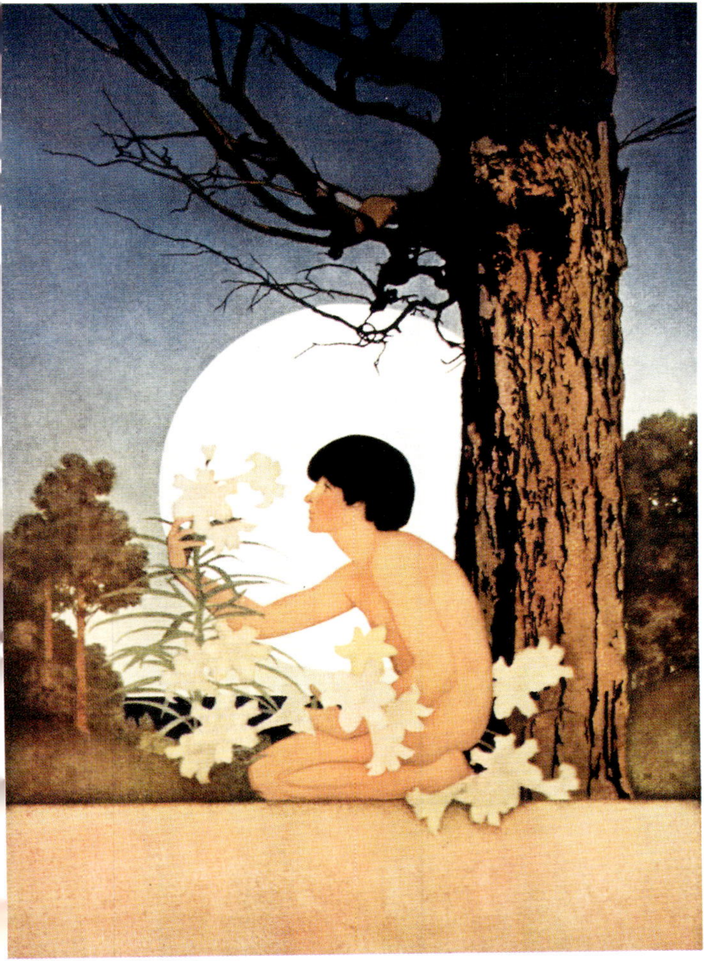

Vignettes

es Vignettes Vignet
Vignettes Vignettes
es Vignettes Vignet
Vignettes Vignettes
es Vignettes Vignet
Vignettes Vignettes
es Vignettes Vignet
Vignettes Vignettes
es Vignettes Vignet
Vignettes Vignettes
Vignettes Vignett